Sister Mary, the Baker, the Barber and the Bricklayer

By

Jeffrey T. Mitchell, Ph.D.

And

William "Josey" L. Visnovske

Dedication

To Kyla Brigid and Angela Faith, my two greatest blessings. My heart jumps when you come into view. You light up a room, a house, and my world. You are my joy, my hope and my love. You will always live in my heart.

- Jeffrey T. Mitchell –

Dedication

To my mom, to Sara, my wife, and my boys for being there as I try to find that balance between my love of them and my love of God and Country. To John, Eric, and Jeff for the support in making me who I am as I walk down this path that was not the plan. For our military and our emergency services personnel who make me realize my struggles are not struggles, just life.

- William "Josey" L. Visnovske -

Contents

INTRODUCTION

When I walked into the restaurant over six years ago and met Dr. Mitchell for the first time, I had no idea of the journey we would begin there. We had spoken on the phone several times and he had agreed to help me with my research on the impact of fatality fires on fire investigators. I remember sitting there and wondering how his city streets of Brooklyn, NY and my back woods hills and swamps could ever coexist in the same world.

Only a month before our meeting, I did not know he existed and I knew nothing about Critical Incident Stress Management. As we broke bread, I learned how different we were. I also learned that what had bonded us before we even met was our need to help others. I also learned that we both loved being a parent.

We spent the next few years doing the research and, once again, I saw how different we were. He would introduce me to his world and, after he put about a gallon of bug spray on himself, I would introduce him to mine. The differences were very apparent. Our passion, however, to help others built a bond between us.

We completed the research and then he said we should write a book. I must admit the book idea was not one I was interested in but I went along with it. The research brought attention to me and to be honest I did not like that. The research, however, did help people so I thought the book might help too. We called the book, *Crucial Moments: Stories of Support in Times of Crisis.*

During the last six years, I pursued several instructor certificates in Critical Incident Stress Management. I cannot say I enjoyed teaching because it requires me to be a more public person than I like. There seems to be at least one student in every class who is helped by something he or she learned in the course. Knowing I have taught something that eased another's pain has caused me to positively change my attitude about teaching. Now I actually like teaching those courses. It is still not easy for a very private person like me, who spent six years in undercover law enforcement work, to be that open to other people. Teaching makes you more vulnerable and, simultaneously, it helps people. I like that part.

Dr. Mitchell has routinely taken me out of my small comfort zone and showed me that there are many ways to help people. Sometimes we have to step outside our world to connect with others. Sometimes we must share our pain, our struggles, and be willing to be criticized for our genuine efforts to help others. Again, in order to help, I have to expose a large part of me.

This second co-authored book was my idea. Many of the stories in this book were written for you the reader. Since I was 12, I wrote for me and tucked those stories in a box. Only a few people I selected were allowed to read them. Now I write many stories for you.

Through Dr. Mitchell's guidance I have seen the different ways I can help people. Before starting this book, I went to him with a list of recurring issues and themes I frequently see when trauma finds its way to people I meet. I wanted him to write the detailed commentaries that would provide insights into the stories. I wanted him to help people understand trauma and provide guidelines for recovering from traumatic stress. In the pages to come, you will read things that I have felt, seen, heard, and tasted, and some are so vivid they will be with me forever. In the last six years, I have been privileged to educate people about how trauma attacks us, how it works in our minds, and how it lingers in our souls. The reactions from the people I meet gave me passion and energy to proceed on this journey with Dr. Mitchell.

Our job is not to make people feel better but, to help people find answers or, at least, some relief from a traumatic event. I wanted a book that people could read to help them understand and process a terrible event that has happened or horrible events that are yet to come. I wanted a book that would cover not just the big, news worthy events but the every day events that are big to us and may mean nothing to others.

Dr. Mitchell and I have somehow combined our two worlds and besides his concrete and my swamp waters those are really the only things that separate us anymore. As we continue this journey, we progress forward in search of a better understanding of the events that stick with us. We will never have all the answers. It is clear to us now that our lives came together to help people like you and ourselves to look for those answers.

The Book's Structure

This book has a very distinctive feature. There are both story chapters and commentary chapters. A commentary chapter follows each true story and bears the same number as the story. The commentary chapters provide comments, remarks, interpretations, and explanations related to the story. In addition, commentary chapters provide information about the brain and how it processes traumatic events.

Chapter 1
Story Power

From cave paintings to the development of language and from the Greek tragedies to the invention of the printing press and all the way to modern movies, humans have had a need to tell stories. Whether written or spoken, stories are important. Stories help us to interpret nature. Stories are important to understand and maintain our history and traditions; they inform, warn, instruct, educate, guide, and influence human behavior. They bond us to relatives and friends. They entertain, thrill, uplift, and inspire us. Stories are even crucial for the maintenance of our mental and physical health. Stories instill hope, faith, courage, respect, and human resilience. Stories have the power to heal us emotionally and physically. There is power in the story, both for the listener and for the storyteller.

Every person has at least one story that needs to be told. When stories are told, especially when they are heard or read by others who understand, the listeners and storyteller can experience growth and change. Even untold stories have an influence on us. Untold stories can bind up our energy. They block us from being our best. Untold stories leave us depressed, sleep-deprived, lacking in confidence, frustrated, isolated, frightened, and confused. They also make us angry and resentful, distracted, self-absorbed and very difficult to live with. Untold stories equals unexpressed emotions. Unexpressed emotions can become a threat to our immune system and to our physical and mental health.

James W. Pennebaker is a Professor of Psychology at the University of Texas at Austin. He is a pioneer in the use of expressive writing to help with healing. After studying the effects of telling or writing one's experiences he authored the book, *Writing to Heal* (2004). When a person can turn their experiences into a story and express it, his or her immune system is strengthened. Students found improvements in their grades. People found that the expression of their stories improved the quality of their lives. Pennebaker found that although telling the story to another person had significant positive health benefits, it wasn't always necessary to actually tell the story. The writing of a story about one's personal loss or tragedy had powerful health benefits as well (Griffith, 2005).

Pennebaker does not recommend writing a journal every day. He cautions us against becoming absorbed in self pity if we write about the same traumatic experience too often and for too long a period of time (beyond a few weeks). He recommends writing for 20 minutes for each of 4 days. He suggests that people write about their deepest emotions and thoughts. They should write how the experience has influenced and altered aspects of their lives including career, family, and relationships. Writing one's thoughts and feelings about an experience helps us to focus and to step back and evaluate what is really important in our lives. Then we can decide if we need to make any changes for ourselves. Pennebaker says that people who can organize a story out of their experience, thoughts, and feelings benefit more than people who don't (Griffith, 2005).

Pennebaker's guidelines for writing about one's life experiences are to write in a place and at a time when you won't be distracted and write for 20 minutes continuously. He suggests that writers disregard spelling and grammar while they are writing their thoughts and feelings. It is important that writers write for themselves. Each person should write about something personally intense and important. Pennebaker finally cautions people to only write about things they can handle at the time they are writing and postpone things that are still emotionally overwhelming (Griffith, 2005). Sometimes, putting the writing aside and then looking at it later may help the person to see if their perspectives are changing or if they can make a story out of the thoughts and emotions they wrote about earlier.

The story can set one's emotions free and bring about healing and a new, healthier, perspective on life and the people we care about and who care about us. Story telling frees up our love – for somebody or something in our lives.

When someone has a story to tell, care enough to listen. When someone cares enough to listen, tell your story.

Vive Griffith (2005). "Writing to Heal: feature story." University of Texas, Office of Public Affairs (March 15, 2005).

James W. Pennebaker (2004). *Writing to Heal: A guided journal for recovering from trauma & emotional upheaval.* Oakland, CA: New Harbinger Publications.

- JTM -

Follow–up to Chapter 1
Got a Story to Tell?

If you have ever wanted to write a short, true story about one of your experiences, but fear no one would want to read it, give us a try. We promise to take your story seriously. Write your story and send a hard copy to Dr. Jeff Mitchell or Josey Visnovske. Send it to us at:

Dr. Jeff Mitchell / Josey Visnovske
P.O. Box 1789
Ellicott City, Maryland 21041

We will read it and one of us will write a brief response back to you. Here are several guidelines for your stories.

1. Send a hard copy (on paper) because we receive so many emails we are afraid your story will be lost among the 800 or more emails we receive each week.
2. Avoid any information in your story that would identify a specific person.
3. Your story can be about almost any topic: peace, war, facing evil, struggling, loyalty, courage, suffering, tragedy, self image, recovery, stress, disaster, resilience, loss, rescue, law enforcement, fire operations, emergency medical services, children, growing up, hope, joy, faith, trust, or love.
4. Make sure you include your name, address and phone number so we can get back to you.

- JTM and WLV -

J. T .Mitchell / W. J. Visnovske

Chapter 2

A Boy Named Ben

Ben's father stood there telling us a story about his four year-old son. One night his mother had given Ben a bath and dressed him for bed. She turned her back and Ben ran out of the house in his pajamas into the pigpen to help his dad who was still working. As his father started to scold Ben, Ben told his father, "A man's gotta do what a man's gotta do." I could not help but laugh inside and at that moment I felt I knew Ben; we were cut from the same cloth.

As the bus bounced across the bridge leading to Parris Island I asked myself, "what had I done?" I was 33, married, and had been a police officer for 12 years. I also had a four-year degree, so why at this late age did I feel it was so important for me to join the Marine Corps reserves. I had answered the question several times when people found out I joined but now, as the lights of Parris Island shone through the salty night air, it seemed hard to rationalize what I had done. As the bus came to a stop a tall, fit drill instructor boarded the bus and the fires of hell were unleashed. Like a fiery beast from some deep dark hole he screamed his commands and they echoed in my head. I moved as fast as I could but not fast enough to please him. He screamed in my face and I felt the heat from his lungs. He told us to stand on these gold footprints that were painted on the street. As I stood there I wondered if the Catholic priest that married my wife and me stood on these same footprints. Before he was a priest he was a Sergeant in the Marine Corps during the Vietnam War. I wondered if the Missouri State Trooper who taught me how to work undercover stood on these same footprints. I thought of my father and wondered if any of the Marines that rode on his ship stood on these footprints. All of my heroes had served their country, so maybe that was the reason I felt it was important I join. As the beast continued to yell, I stood there shaking. I had been in tougher spots during my law enforcement career but maybe I was afraid that I could not fill these footprints of all the great men who had gone before me.

Words cannot describe the days that followed my landing on Parris Island. Parris Island is a special place where boys are made into men. A group of men train these boys to fight the good fight and stand tall for their country. I was older than most drill instructors but I still had to learn the Marine Corps way. I had been through five law enforcement academies but none were like this. These men were training us for war. Prior to this, all my training was focused on asking questions. Shooting was always a last resort. In my platoon, I was the oldest by far. The average age on Parris Island was 19. The boys in my platoon all had their own reasons for joining. Some wanted to prove something to someone back home, some wanted to prove something to themselves, and then there were those like me that wanted to serve their country.

A friend told me that when he was on Parris Island the concept of time was strange: it moved like the wind and then it seemed to not move at all. It's hard to explain but he was right. Sometimes the days would fly by and other times the days seemed unbearably long. Unlike my younger counterparts I missed my wife, my job, and being alone. The drill instructors had difficulty teaching the younger ones the importance of teamwork and how we are all connected. The physical training was not that difficult for me because I've always worked out. I injured my elbow and had surgery years before I entered the Marine Corps and, as the weeks went by, my elbow began to hurt. I never said anything to the drill instructors but I would always ice my elbow at night after the lights were out. On April 5, 2002, I marched across the parade deck, the oldest of 362 recruits. As I marched my heroes marched with me. I had become a Marine. As friends and family ran onto the parade deck I held my hand up to block the bright sun so I could see my wife. When I finally saw her we hugged and tears fell from my face.

I reported to my reserve unit and in a few days I was back at my regular job. It took a few weeks to feel normal again but my dream of becoming a Marine was a reality. My elbow continued to hurt, so I saw my doctor. He said I may have re-injured it and gave me some medication. A few months passed and my elbow did not feel any better. I reported the injury to my reserve unit, so I would not injure it worse. I continued to see my doctor and he would report my condition to the reserve unit. I received word that my unit had been activated for the war in Iraq but I was being processed for a medical discharge. I think back to 1990. I started my career as a deputy sheriff in Missouri. I debated then joining the Marine Corps to help fight the war in Iraq but felt I should stay with law enforcement. Now my country was once again going to war with Iraq and, again, I was staying with law enforcement.

On November 7, 2003, I was packing my bags in a hotel preparing to return home after a law enforcement trip. I saw on the television that a Black Hawk helicopter had been shot down in Iraq. No names were listed, just that six soldiers had been killed. I sat on the edge of the bed and said my morning prayer. My father gave me this Catholic prayer card and every morning I say the prayer. I don't claim to be a real religious man but I say one prayer everyday. I prayed for the soldiers who were shot down and the ones who continue to fight. I stepped on the elevator and by the time I landed on the ground floor I had forgotten about the soldiers and my thoughts were on my drive home.

As I was driving home my wife called me on my cell phone. She informed that her cousin was the pilot of the Black Hawk. She had been crying and I tried to comfort her but my efforts failed over the phone. I had met her cousin once when he was in Black Hawk pilot school. He was a big kid from north Missouri. I have referred to his family as the "corn-fed cousins." The part of Missouri they are from is known for big deer from eating all the corn that is grown up there. I guess those cousins ate a lot of corn because they were also big. We were already planning to go to

13

Missouri because twice a year I go to Missouri to hunt deer and turkey with my childhood friend.

On November 9, 2003, my wife and I had tickets to see Alan Jackson in concert. Some of his songs made us smile but others reminded us of the war in Iraq. Sitting in front of us was a young man who had too much to drink and he asked me if I was in the military. I guess he thought that because of my haircut. I told him I was in the Marine Corps reserves. He leaned back and said, "Thanks." I wished my wife's cousin were there to hear those words, not me. I had not done anything to deserve anyone's thanks.

On November 10, 2003, I went to work and wore my Marine Corps polo shirt to honor the Marine Corps on their birthday. In the mail that same day I received my medical discharge papers. As I read the words I thanked God for at least letting me be a Marine for three months.

As my wife and I drove to Missouri we tried to pretend it was our usual trip but the death of her cousin made this trip a sad one. We drove through Fort Campbell and my wife started to cry. She said this is where her cousin's body was being shipped. I asked my wife if I ever told her about my theory on life's eight seconds. She said, "no." I told my wife that to me life is about eight seconds. We all have eight seconds and in those eight seconds we will do something that will change history forever. We might wish our eight seconds will save a nation but in reality our eight seconds might be something as simple as making someone smile. Our eight seconds might be letting someone out in traffic because if they would have waited, two blocks later they would have been involved in a accident and been killed. They would have left behind a child who would have found a cure for cancer but, now won't because his mother is dead and life has no meaning to him. I further explained to my wife that we are all one big puzzle helping each other make the pieces fit. Some of us must go before the others so the puzzle will continue to grow. I further explained his eight seconds may have been when he was a child or maybe moments before the Black Hawk went down. As hard as it is to understand the death of anyone, I guaranteed her that her cousin had his eight seconds and generations to come will benefit from his eight seconds.

In the chapel, my wife leaned over to me and asked me if I needed a tissue. I told her no and listened to Ben's father talk more about his son. I also listened to schoolteachers, friends, and family talk about a boy named Ben. As the casket passed us, my wife and I felt the cold north Missouri air fill the room as the doors opened. We walked outside and what I saw restored my faith, not in God, but in our country. The streets were lined with people holding American flags. The town had shut down and everyone was there holding a flag. School buses were parked where children were brought in to show their respect to a fallen soldier. Businesses were closed and the owners and workers stood on the street holding flags. As we followed the funeral procession I could not believe what my eyes were seeing. In this town of 2500 people, all 2500 must have been on the street that day. I did not always agree with the decisions made by the people who sit behind a shinny oak desk but I would never turn my back on my country like some generations have. In recent years I must admit I had lost faith in our nation. Seeing these people who don't even wear a uniform stand tall for their country was a breath of fresh air.

As they pulled the casket from the hearse, all the soldiers standing around saluted. I thought maybe I should salute but I was only a Marine for three months. We followed the casket to the grave sight walking past Veterans of Foreign Wars who saluted the casket. The veterans were old and older and none as young as the boy named Ben. As Taps was played and the 21-gun salute was fired my hand was drawn to my forehead and I stood tall to salute a fallen soldier. As the shots rang out the deer had nothing to fear for everyone there cringed as the shots echoed across the cornfields. I stood there and noticed a little boy in front of me holding his arms around his father's leg. The boy waved at me as I finished my salute. I waved back and prayed his eight seconds will not come for some time.

The day after the funeral I was in the woods with my childhood friend hunting deer. It was a cold rainy day and I wished I were somewhere warmer. Around noon the rain took a break and we decided to look for deer across a field. We were talking about the days when we used to play war games in the thicket of woods next to the field. We would buy old surplus military clothes and pretend to be soldiers in war. I realized I was still wearing surplus military clothing but some of it I wore during the three months I was a Marine. In the thicket grew some berries called Hackberries and we used them as bullets. I could not help but wonder if the boy named Ben did the same thing growing up. As we stood there talking about the old days, I looked at the top of a big old Oak tree that stood in the middle of the thicket. I pulled the binoculars to my eyes and to my surprise there was a bald eagle. I handed the binoculars to my friend and he confirmed it was a bald eagle. I asked him if he had ever seen a bald eagle out here. He said, "Not in my thirty six years." We stood there for several minutes watching the eagle watch us. Then he lifted off and spread his six-foot wingspan and flew away. I watched him fly into the distance and I guess it started to rain again because I felt water on my face. The eagle made me realize that a cold rainy day with your friend is better than no day at all.

As we walked away from the field I thought about the boy named Ben. I thought about how some people said his death was a waste. I believe his death was not a waste but a tragedy. If his death makes us love more, slow down and realize we are all in this together, then how can that be a waste? If his death inspires just one of those children on the side of the street to become something great or just inspires the child to be a good person, then how can that be a waste? If his death reminds a guy like me that I'm not bullet proof, then how can that be a waste?

The clock in the truck says it's 4:51 am. My wife and I are driving back to the place we call home. Twice a year we return to Missouri and twice a year we put two American flags on mile marker 134 on Interstate 55 in Perry County Missouri. Almost twenty years ago a Missouri State Trooper was killed there doing what a man's gotta do. I never knew him but I refuse to let his death be a waste. As the highway rolls under us, my mind wanders back to that place where the boy named Ben is buried.

By now the smoke from the 21-gun salute has disappeared into the cornfields of north Missouri. The trampled down grass around the gravesite has risen back up. The deer in the fields next to the cemetery will once again cringe at the sound of gunfire. As we drive into the early morning hours the sun rises and Alan sings us a song about, "that'll be alright." Ben's death will never be all right but it will be okay if we, as a society, do not let his death be a waste. He did for the army what a man's gotta do. It doesn't matter if we remember Ben as a son, a brother, a husband, a cousin, or a soldier, as long as we remember the boy named Ben.

Written in memory of Captain Ben Smith and for all the fine patriotic people of Monroe City, Missouri. May God watch over you!

- WLV -

Comments on Chapter 2

Birds of a Feather

My mother frequently used a phrase when I was a child. It was, *"Birds of a feather flock together."* If I use it on my own children now, it draws peculiar stares as if I had suddenly developed six heads. If I try to explain it as my mother had explained it to me, the stares continue. The six heads are still there. Let me try the explanation with you anyway. Maybe it will make sense. Maybe I won't have six heads to you.

My mother always used the expression to warn me that the friends I choose to hang around with would indicate to everyone in the world who I really was. She noted that sparrows hung around with other sparrows and pigeons could always be found with other pigeons. Likewise robins could be found with other robins (birds with the same feathers). You got it? She would go on the say if I hung with good kids, people would see me as a good kid and if I hung out with bad kids, people would believe I was a bad kid because, as birds of the same feather always stayed with their own kind, kids would choose to be with kids who were the most like themselves. Stay with me, now. I am working on a point here.

Triggers

When it comes to traumatic thoughts about tragedies, pain, death, grief, and loss, those memories are like birds of the same feather. They tend to clump together because they all have something negative about them. Pain in life or the memory of the death of one person **triggers** memories of other painful experiences or the deaths of people we loved. Traumatic memories trigger other traumatic memories. Pain attracts more painful thoughts.

A **trigger** can cause a gun to fire. In like manner, one thought can trigger the brain and stir up more memories.

18

In Josey's story about the boy named Ben, certain triggers caused other traumatic or painful memories to come to the surface. His brain quickly goes to the Marine Corps heroes who went before him at Parris Island. Then onto his dad. Then comes the death of soldiers on a Blackhawk helicopter. The death of his wife's cousin, Ben, who was the pilot on that helicopter, eventually connects him to the death of a Missouri State Trooper who was doing "what a man's gotta do." That reminds him of Ben's funeral.

There are a number of triggers that are apparent in the story. Ben's words, "a man's gotta do what a man's gotta do" is one of the numerous triggers in the story. Other triggers are people wearing uniforms – marines, police officers, army personnel, his Dad during the war. Salutes, bullets, mile marker 134 on Interstate 55 in Missouri, and even hackberries draw in other traumatic memories.

Nobdy can tolerate a steady diet of painful memories. Thankfully our systems can figure out when we need a break from all the painful memories that have flocked together. Some of those painful memories can also trigger some positive, even enjoyable memories. Examples in the story are deer hunting, a break in the rain, hackberries, humor by Ben's dad at his funeral, the kindness of the town's people who freeze framed their day for a few minutes to pay tribute to a fallen local soldier-hero.

- JTM -

CHAPTER 3
The Buckle

I strapped my cooler to my bike and rode through the pine thicket on our driveway. As I came to the top of the hill that led to the creek, I held on as I coasted down. I made it almost half way up the next hill before I had to push my way to the top. I parked my bike in the woods and walked my way up to the county gravel road. I stood there in the dark with my cooler in hand and soon my ride pulled up with the dust following the truck as it came to a stop. A man who lived down the road would give me a ride to the 5,000-acre farm I was working on. The man had a long last name that started with a 'P' so my best friend, who lived across the county gravel road from me, decided we would call him Pinky. I'm pretty sure the man had no clue we called him Pinky. The ride to the 5000-acre farm was about 15 miles and he would drop me off and I would walk about a ¼ mile to the farm. After I would work a full day he would pick me up and drop me off at my driveway.

Pinky was an average man who did not say much but made it possible for me to work on that farm before I had my driver's license.

On Saturdays I did not work at the farm. I would go to town with mom to shop for groceries. The store was located in a strip of stores and at the one end was a gun store. Mom would shop for groceries and I would stay in the gun store and look at guns. One Saturday, as the bell on the door rang as I walked into the gun store, I saw what I thought was a cartoon character. A tall slender man, with a ten-gallon cowboy hat on and a belt buckle the size of a dinner plate, stood behind the counter. The man had a big mustache and a smile that told me he was real. I was scared of him, but curious to see if he was real. I walked up to the counter

21

and he said, "You wanna look at a gun partner?" I said, "No sir I'm just looking." Before the words left my mouth his hand shot out like a bullet and he said, "My name is G-Man, what's yours?" In a somewhat timid voice I said "Leroy" and he said, "Nice to meet you Laroy." I was not about to correct him for calling me Laroy and not Leroy but I shook his hand. I was so mesmerized by his hat, mustache and belt buckle I failed to see the small fingerless leather gloves he was wearing. I felt the rough leather against my hand and his grip was strong. The handshake ended and I felt like I had just grabbed a hold of a tornado but one that never really hurt anyone.

I continued to work that summer on the farm. The farm had enclosed tractors that meant being in air conditioning. Our home had no air conditioning and our tractors at home were not enclosed so, when I could, I avoided the enclosed tractors. I loved being able to smell the fresh soil and feel the heat from the tractor. I liked the smell of the diesel fuel being burned and hearing the tractor run. Sometimes I would get dropped off at a 500 acre field along a big river and spend all day with the tractor, the field, my cooler, and never see another person. Those were the best days.

My trips to the gun store became more frequent and soon I was not afraid of the G-Man. One Saturday, parked on the sidewalk in front of the gun store, was a Harley. The Harley had a "chopper" front end and something told me it belonged to the G-Man. I asked him about the Harley and he said, "It's mine." He asked me if I ride and I said, "I have a dirt bike I ride on the farm." He said, "Well one day, young Laroy, you will have to ride a Harley."

The gun store was a collection of characters that I never read about in any of the books they made us read in school. One Saturday I followed G-Man to the gravel parking lot behind the store. About 25 yards behind the back door was a large old stump. At the back door stood a tall man, ten-gallon cowboy hat, large dinner plate belt buckle, and black cowboy boots with silver tips on the tips of the boots. The man raised a Colt Model 1911 45-caliber pistol and fired a few rounds into the stump. I stood there trying to figure out how it was ok to shoot a pistol in the city limits but G-Man said, "Well Hacksaw, how did she shoot?" The man who I now figured out was called Hacksaw said, "She is a tack driver, I will take her." Hacksaw looked at me and said, "Who are you?" G-Man said, "This is my young partner Laroy." Hacksaw shook my hand and said, "Nice to meet you Laroy," and once again I was not about to correct them for calling me Laroy.

One Saturday G-Man took me to his shop and rolled out his 1957 Harley Sportster and said, "If you can start it, young Laroy, you can ride it." The Harley was a kick-start and I was not really heavy enough to kick start it but I tried. After about 30 minutes, and a very sore leg, it started. G-Man walked over and handed me his helmet and leather jacket. None of it fit. He said, "Take her down the road, partner, you earned it." I told the G-Man I did not have a driver's license and he simply said, "Ain't no big deal and young boys gotta ride."

I knew it was wrong but it felt so right. I rolled down the two-lane road past fresh cut hay fields and felt every bump from the asphalt. G-Man's leather jacket blasted against my body and his helmet was bouncing around on my head. I was scared I would get in trouble but I knew what an honor it was for G-Man to let me ride his bike so I lived in the moment. The ride was something that could not be described in words and that day changed me. As I rolled back up to G-Man's shop, he was smiling like I had never seen him smile. In his loud voice he hollered, "Well, young Laroy, did ya peel some rubber off that tire?" I smiled and said "No, I just took her down the road." I was never big on keeping secrets from my parents but, I thought, I might just forget to mention that day.

When the summer was over I continued my friendship with G-Man and from time to time Hacksaw would make his appearance. Hacksaw was more reserved than G-Man but he too took an interest in me. G-Man would tell me how to do something and Hacksaw would tune it down a bit. I invited G-Man out to the house to meet my parents. My mom made chili and we watched the G-Man wash his fingertips at our kitchen sink because he

Sister Mary, the Baker, the Barber, and the Bricklayer

always wore his fingerless gloves. He took his cowboy hat off and hung it on his chair and blessed the meal. He entertained us with stories of hunting out west and his energy poured through the house. My father, a quiet man, sat there and watched the G-Man. I think a part of my dad was thinking 'what the hell did you drag home?' and the other part was 'this man has manners and blessed the meal so it could be worse.'

That winter I turned 16 and knew that I needed a vehicle. G-Man had a nice 1970 four door black Lincoln Continental and he made me an offer I could not refuse. I could barely see over the steering wheel when I drove through the pine thicket and into the field behind our house. My dad stood there as I got out and shook his head. He simply said "You need to get something good on gas because we live 25 miles from town." A few weeks later I traded the Lincoln Continental for a black Harley and when I rode through the pine thicket with the loud exhaust sounding like a dying tractor my dad just shook his head. My dad made a spot for the Harley in our garage so I knew he accepted it but he never told me that.

I got a job at a grocery store in town so I rode the Harley to school and after school I would go to work. The rides were cold but Hacksaw gave me a leather jacket and leather pants to keep me warm. I worked every day after school and weekends. I was not supposed to work full time but I did. My grades in school suffered but even when I was in class my mind drifted to the being on the Harley or being with G-Man and Hacksaw. Even though they were older than me I seem to fit in with them better than most of the kids I went to school with. I knew my dad accepted my love of Harley's when he cosigned a loan for one at the bank and I had two in the garage and his truck sat outside.

When I graduated high school my parents encouraged me to go to college but I said I did not want to go. Hacksaw said if I did not go we would no longer be friends so I went to a junior college. I got a job at a store in the same strip of stores that the now closed gun store used to be in. I parked my Harley on the sidewalk just like G-Man did years before. I applied myself more at college

24

than high school and maybe because I was taking courses I liked or I was paying for it.

When I told my dad I wanted to be a police officer he just shook his head but said I'm glad you are going to college. My dad worked in a rock quarry and hated his job of destroying the earth, so he did not want me to become like him.

As the college years passed I soon found myself with an offer to be a police officer away from home. I found my dad in the barn and asked him what I should do. He said "If you don't leave I will ask you to leave, a nest is not meant to live in just be raised in." I took the job offer and packed my stuff up. Dad handed me a letter and said when you get there read this. When I got to my apartment that had air conditioning that I did not turn on, I opened the letter. Dad wrote: "You were the last to leave and I waited for the day to have a bathroom to myself, no Harleys in the garage, your heavy work-out bags out of the barn, and peace and quiet." He wrote: "I walked up to the barn and sat down on a tire and cried when I saw all your stuff gone." He wrote: "I never hated the Harleys or you being a police officer I just did not want you to die." I sat in my apartment surrounded by boxes and never felt so alone. Dad really cared. I could just not see that because he never said much.

The next few years I saw G-Man and Hacksaw but not like it was before I went to work as a police officer. I was out of the nest and living the life of an undercover police officer. I kept my Harley at another police officer's house some 50 miles away from my undercover apartment. I enjoyed the 3-hour rides in the middle of the night when I could sneak away and find my way back to that pine thicket that surrounded my parents' home. I think my father could see the toll of the life I had chosen. I had a post office box in another town under a different name and dad would send me these post cards. He titled it Living Beyond the Sidewalks. He would speak of the earth and our role here and anything that crossed his mind. He would sign off by calling it Outhouse Philosophy. I never saw this side of dad until I moved away but his depth amazed me. Those postcards kept me from going crazy and I lived to check that post office for them. I still have those cards to this day.

I stood there in my Marine Corps uniform with my wife and sons by my side. Across the room my mom greeted people as they entered the VFW hall to pay respects to my father. Outside I heard the rumble of a Harley and then entered the G-Man. He was dressed in leather and had that smile on. Our eyes locked and soon we hugged each other. My boys looked at G-Man like I did many years ago. He said, "When did you become a Marine young Laroy?" I said, "I've been busy since I moved away and I would like you to meet my family." G-Man was in his purest form and my boys were mesmerized. When I moved away G-Man took really good care of my parents so he came today to make sure dad got the respect he earned. I told G-Man that when we knew dad had around six months to live I would ride my Harley 650 miles back and forth to help mom. We laughed together thinking back to that first Harley I brought home and how dad shook his head.

My father's death brought G-Man and me back to life, or maybe it was the way my boys looked at him and every young boy needs a role model besides his daddy. When we would come to visit my mom, it was now routine for G-Man to join us for supper. One time G-Man was supposed to meet us at Mom's but we got delayed. When we finally got there G-Man was cooking on the grill in the back yard. G-Man said, "I figured you all got hung up so I made myself at home and took some meat out of the freezer." Mom looked at me and said, "The house was locked." I laughed and said, "Well he is the G-Man."

When you move away from home your first reaction when the phone rings is to look at caller id and see if this call is going to be good or bad. Mom called to tell me she heard G-Man had cancer and was real sick but was hiding out somewhere. I stayed in touch with Hacksaw but not like I should have. I called him about G-Man. He was very appreciative and he said, "I will find him." A few days later Hacksaw called to tell me he found G-Man and he was real sick but was going to get some treatments. Hacksaw and I shared some stories and I told him next time I was in town I would look him up. I told him I nicknamed my oldest son 'Hacksaw'.

G-Man got treatments for the cancer and we saw him on our next visit to my mom's. The tornado in him I saw years ago was gone. He told us, "They cut a thing out of me the size of possum." Whatever they cut out of him took a part of his spark, the part that attracted folks to him. My boys had to show him their cowboy boots and belt buckles and then I could see a brief glimmer of his spark, but like a shooting star it was gone.

Awhile later, the phone rang. It was Mom again. I could tell it was bad. She said, "Hacksaw died, I'm sorry." I was expecting to hear about G-Man, not Hacksaw. I recalled that day when he told me he had some form of cancer from the Agent Orange that they sprayed in the war. I was just a teenager when he told me that. Cancer was a word that meant nothing to me then. Now when I hear the word my mind fills with pictures of those that cancer has taken from me. Hacksaw had said that between the medicine and treatments he could no longer wear cowboy boots and that was what he hated the most. I guess after twenty some odd years, Hacksaw was tired of wearing tennis shoes.

I sat there and looked up at his picture hanging on the wall and the rush of emotions that came with that news attempted to fill every void in my soul. The times we shot together, the times we rode together but most of all the times he guided me to become a man. I've never been big on funerals and really don't understand them so I told mom I would not be attending. Mom said she would go with G-Man and pass on my respects. After the funeral, Mom called to tell me that at the gravesite G-Man took out his pistol after the service was over and, in G-Man fashion, fired a few rounds for his old partner Hacksaw.

A few weeks later I went to visit Mom and went to Hacksaw's house to see his stepson. I had not seen Hacksaw's stepson in 30 years. We were greeted with open arms. On the refrigerator, there was a picture I had sent Hacksaw of my family. The stepson went on and on about how his dad spoke of me. It was then that I realized Hacksaw was proud of me as well as the man I had become. As we were leaving I asked the stepson if I could I have one of his dad's dog tags and he said, "hold on." He came back and said "dad would want you to have it." When I got back in the truck I placed the dog tag on a ring I have with other dog tags and religious medals of my fallen heroes.

A few days later I took a rifle I got from Hacksaw when I was 16 and shot a hole through a quarter at 100 yards. I mailed the quarter to his stepson and simply said thanks.

A few months later I was in a big city preparing to do a presentation to 400 people from around the world on an subject some feel I know what I'm talking about but, if you ask me, I'm as clueless as that 15 year old without a driver's license. I was giving the presentation with a friend of mine who has done this kind of thing a lot more than me. At the last minute I left and sent a text to my friend that I had to get a different suit. By a miracle I found a western store and bought boots, a western suit, and a big Marine Corps belt buckle. My friend called in a panic and asked, "Where are you" and I said, "On my way back." When I walked up to my friend he looked at me and shook his head. I said, "If we are going to continue doing this stuff then I need to be me and this is who I am." He smiled and said, "I wish I could get away with wearing that."

Months later, I was standing in the middle of a four-story building that had collapsed. I was doing my job as a certified fire investigator. My phone rang. I attempted to remove my hardhat, respirator, and sunglasses to answer it but I was too slow. The caller id said it was Mom calling. I walked out of the rubble and called Mom. She said, "The cancer came back on G-Man and he has died." I told Mom I would not be attending any service because I had to complete my mission but please pass on my respects. I put my gear back on and went back into the rubble. A few hours later a man I had only known a few days yelled at me through his respirator and asked if I was ok. I said, "Yes." I'm not sure what he saw through the hardhat, respirator, and sunglasses, but he saw or felt something.

At my request my mom asked G-Man's family for one of his belt buckles and something to put on my dog tag/medal ring. The package came in the mail and I opened it. I knew what was in the box before I opened it but some things we just cannot be prepared for. As I lifted the belt buckle and belt from the box my knees got weak and I felt sick. My head spun and I felt desperate. It was as if I had voids opening up in my soul and at that moment nothing could fill them. How the hell could I be holding the G-Man belt buckle? Where is the tall bulletproof man who wore this buckle? How did he get away before I could say good-bye? In the bottom of the box was a necklace he wore and the voids only got worse when I saw it. I walked into the house and placed them in a drawer next to my Marine Corps belt buckle and have not looked at them since. I called my mom and thanked her and I said, "I cannot study this too much right now."

It's been several months since the G-Man died and every time I crack the throttle on my Harley I drift back to that two-lane road where it all began. The leather pants I got from Hacksaw hang in a closet and the jacket has been on loan to my friend down the road. The gear I wear now when I ride is fancy and should keep some skin on me if I go down. I'm 47 years old and I've owned a Harley since I was 16 but I don't own a Harley t-shirt or have a Harley sticker on my Jeep. Most people don't even know I own a Harley. A Harley is at the core of who I am and is better therapy than any drug, alcohol, or doctor. My first ride on a Harley was like being on a fast tractor but with more wind.

I can relive those moments on the tractor and the Harley, but I cannot touch the hero's that have passed on. All I can do is remember them. My first hero was my father—the quiet man who later on in life showed me his depth and love in written words on a postcard to a fictitious person. There was Sister Mary who gave me the crucifix that her mother kissed every night before bed. She gave me the crucifix because she believed in me when very few did. Then there was Frank, who I wrote about in another story, a Marine who also was a cowboy. Then G-Man, Hacksaw, and my catholic priest that carried a Colt 45 and he too was a Marine. My wife became my hero when I saw her give birth to our boys. I don't think my mom was my hero until she held my father and he took his last breath and somehow she found the strength to go on with life. I could write for hours about the men and women who have influenced my life or inspired me to strive on. Some have no clue what they did for me but their lives affected me.

When I moved away I used to say I was making a difference in the path I had chosen, but now I do not see that. Now what I see is I'm doing my part and that is what I teach my boys. Though we would all love to believe our part is something big and bold, it might not be. The reality is none of us know what our part is so we should give our part every chance we get. We get tunnel vision on what we perceive as success when in reality it might just be a 15-year old boy who is not sure where he fits in. There are those who would not speak fondly of the G-Man's lifestyle but he took the time to help mold me. Hacksaw fine-tuned me. Heroes and role models play a vital part in the development of our youth. Kids need to be inspired by something that is real. Something they can feel like a rough leather glove or the spark of life that can only be felt and never described. I'm guilty of getting lost in what is important and what really matters. My boys inspire me to be a better man but in my pursuit of balance I forget the hero they desperately need. Death has its way of slowing things down and pointing out the voids we all carry around.

The other day it was hot and I told my oldest that he could wear shorts with his cowboy boots instead of his Wranglers and even the G-Man did that. My oldest, aka Hacksaw, smiled and said, "Daddy I'm not that kind of guy." So with his John Deer belt buckle, Wranglers, boots, and cowboy hat he crawled up on the tractor. His younger brother, aka Coyote Bob, crawled up on the tractor with his bucking bull belt buckle, cargo shorts, and hiking boots. Before long I could smell the burning diesel fuel and the wind lifts the front of my cowboy hat and for a brief moment I was 15 and back on the farm.

G-Man had many sayings but only one really fits here. After I would tell G-Man something he would take a deep breath and bellow out "**What a story!**" I agree with G-Man. This was one hell of a story but, if I do my part, this is just another chapter in the book of life. The story of G-Man and Hacksaw is a true story with many parts that are better told around a camp-fire and under the stars that don't judge but have been a source of direction for travelers since this life book started.

I hope that one day my time here will have influenced the lives of others in a positive way and they too can add to this story. No story is perfect but I believe, if we try and do our part at every chance we get, most stories will end as they should. Those that touch and inspire our lives never fade into the sunset but linger in our thoughts as we roll down a two-lane road or smell the burning diesel. The stories of their lives, the things they said; the things they did may get exaggerated over time, but how they influenced our lives never changes. My heroes will always be cowboys. I'm drawn to the hat, the boots, the Wranglers, and, most of all, the buckle. I've lost a lot of heroes the last few years and my ring of dog tags and medals keeps growing. I've also come to realize that if you slow down enough you will never run out of heroes even if they are younger, more innocent belt-buckle-wearing versions of Hacksaw and G-Man. In my case I call these younger versions, young Hacksaw and Coyote Bob.

- WLV -

Comments on Chapter 3

Senses: Hear the Sound, See the Sight, Smell the Smell

A mark of a good writer is when the storyteller can help the reader experience the various sounds, smells, sights, tastes and sensations in the story. Josey is particularly adept at writing the five senses into his stories. His sensory descriptions of the sound of a Harley, or the smell of the soil or sensing a hot tractor engine or seeing the dust that follows a truck on a gravel county road enrich each story. His sensory images also indicate the power of the senses to produce emotional and cognitive reactions. Josey has lived the stories he tells and he is well aware of how our senses and traumatic experiences are forever intimately linked to our thoughts and emotions once they occur in close proximity to each other.

Stress is a very sensory experience. It is not just a psychological occurrence. Our cognitive and emotional interpretations of our experiences are only one part of a stress reaction. Sights, smells, tastes, sounds, and touch are all integral aspects of stress. **The basic definition of stress is a state of physical and psychological arousal**. The more horrible, terrible, awful, threatening, and grotesque an experience is, the greater is the potential that our senses will be triggered, not only at the time of the traumatic event, but far into the future as well.

It works in two ways. Some sights, sounds, odors, tastes or skin sensations can change our thoughts or emotions. For example, a song on the radio may remind us of a person who died and who had loved that song during their life. As a result we may feel sad because we miss that person and their song is playing. The trigger for the emotional reaction is the combination of the sense of hearing and the song that we are hearing. The emotions and thoughts about the person we cared about are linked to the sound of the song.

On the other hand, we can experience some new event that stimulates our senses and then it generates an emotion like fear or grief. The fear, in turn, may bring up the intense memory of a sight, sound, smell, taste, or skin sensation that is not actually present in the environment at the moment.

Here is a good example of how a thought or an emotion can trigger one or more senses to react to the emotion. A good friend of mine was a police officer who was dispatched to a serious auto accident. At the scene he found a twelve-year old girl who had no pulse and was not breathing. He initiated Cardio Pulmonary Resuscitation (CPR). None of his extreme efforts were successful. He was tearful at the scene and for several days later. He was particularly distraught over this child's death because he had a daughter about the same age. When our personal life intersects with our professional life, it is called a **collision of worlds.** (See the explanation of the term collision of worlds below.)

While performing CPR on this severely injured child, blood kept filling her mouth. With almost every breath into the child's lungs, some of that blood got into the mouth of the police officer.

About three months later the officer was dispatched on another serious auto accident. He suddenly had the distressing taste of human blood in his mouth while he was responding. There was no blood present, but he could taste the blood in his mouth. The taste lingered while he was at the scene and dissipated as soon as he cleared the incident.

For a period of twelve years he had the same taste of blood in his mouth whenever he was sent to a serious auto accident. He hated going to accident scenes because the blood taste occurred almost every time.

Psychological Roadmap

One day he told me about the taste of the blood that occurred on deployments to serious auto accidents. After twelve years of this disturbing experience, he felt abnormal, weird, weak, and maybe a bit crazy. When I told him his reaction was, indeed, uncomfortable, but not a sign of weakness or mental disturbance he stared back at me with disbelief. Nobody had ever mentioned that possibility while he was in training to become a police officer. He had never met anyone who had even a similar experience. He had no **psychological road map** to help him understand what was happening to him or how he could overcome this problem. (We will talk about the importance of psychological road maps in the comment section of Chapter 7). He thought that he was mentally unstable. That is why he never mentioned it to me, or anyone else, in all that time.

Eye Movement Desensitization and Re-processing (EMDR)

I sent him to a psychologist who is extremely skilled in providing Eye Movement Desensitization and Reprocessing (EMDR). In two sessions, EMDR helped him to eliminate this distressing sensory response to the very old memory of the death of a child in an auto accident. He told me many times since that he wished he had gone for help a lot earlier.

Now he understood what had happened to him and why it had happened. Taste and smell stimuli come into the brain through nerve pathways that come into extremely close proximity with the amygdala and the hippocampus parts of the brain. Those parts handle the emergency memory system that warns us that we are awfully close to the memory of some traumatic event. The smell or taste can actually be biochemically imprinted on the brain. If a stimulus is present (being deployed on a serious auto accident), the smell and taste of the blood from the previous serious accident instantaneously comes back into memory even if there is no actual blood present. On the other hand, if there is blood present at a scene, even a minor accident, then the memory of tasting the child's blood in the very serious auto accident will come back again.

Once my friend understood what was happening to him, he knew what to do about it and how he could get past it. He had the psychological road map, but only after suffering the distress for a very long time. Pain and distress goes down substantially when accurate, complete and timely information goes up. Understanding what happened to us and why we still react to it makes us free of the torture of inaccurate or incomplete information.

When people do not understand the very intricate and powerful relationship between our senses and our thoughts and feelings they cannot understand how a sound or a visual stimuli or a smell can bring up feelings they hadn't had in years. Some people feel that they may be going insane or that they suffer from some inherent personal weakness. Not true. It may be an uncomfortable, unexpected, and disorienting experience, but it is a very common, natural, and normal occurrence.

The Stress Reaction

A stress reaction is <u>always</u> made up of three essential elements:

1. **Cognitive** interpretations (thoughts)

2. **Emotional** attributes (feelings)

3. **Physical** reactions (body sensations)

These three elements are intertwined with each other. Experience one element and the others will be impacted in one way or another. A thought can generate a feeling and a physical reaction. An emotion can trigger a thought and a physical reaction. A physical sensation can trigger thoughts and feelings. The more severe the original experience, the more closely thoughts, feelings, and physical reactions are interlocked. A mild experience generates mild reactions. Moderate experiences produce somewhat stronger reactions. Severely distressing experiences cause the most intense and most long lasting thoughts, feelings, and physical manifestations of stress.

Collision of Worlds:

A collision of worlds (work world and personal world) can also occur when a child fatality of a fire is wearing the same pajamas as your child wears to bed. It is also a collision of worlds when one's moral code intersects with the necessity to do something one would rather not do. Killing a person to protect one's family members is a classic example. Turning a close family member into law enforcement when the family member has committed a felony crime is another example of the collision of worlds. In this case doing the right thing for the good of the community and for the sake of justice flies against the principle of loyalty to one's family. In such cases we are making decisions against a backdrop of colliding worlds. That is never easy.

- JTM -

J. T .Mitchell / W. J. Visnovske

Chapter 4
My Father's Son

As my mom pulled through the caution light, I knew we were just moments from being at the local military surplus store. The store was located in the center of a mining town that had seen better days. As our old ford pickup truck rolled to a stop, my best friend Dan bailed out of the truck bed. I was right behind him. My mom yelled something but all we heard was the store door close behind us. We ran through the store looking for whatever two young country boys thought they needed to survive. We rummaged through piles of camouflage pants and jackets and wondered if the ones with holes were from the soldiers being shot. We loved being in the surplus store but the store smelled like grandma's closet, so we never stayed in there very long. Dan and I picked out a set of camouflage pants and jackets and I grabbed a green belt that was used to carry a canteen and other gear. My mom paid for our gear and we climbed back in the bed of the truck. As we drove home we removed the soldiers' names from the jackets and wrote our names in with a magic marker.

My mom turned down the gravel road that leads to our houses and the dust rolled into the back of the truck. Dan and I covered our faces with our new jackets to stop the dust from getting into our eyes. The sound of the gravel popping under the tires faded so I knew my mom was turning down the road that we lived on. I removed my jacket from my face and grabbed my BB gun. As we crossed the bridge at the bottom of the hill my mom stopped and Dan and I bailed out with rifles in hand. We crawled under some bushes and put on our new camouflage. I wrapped my new green belt around my waist; I had nothing to attach to it, but it looked cool. We moved across the woods as if the enemy were out there. We had made a training area on the side of the hill and used some old trash that was left from an old homestead to give us targets to shoot at. Dan and I spent many hours each week, training for all the wars we thought we would fight when we got older. No one told us that we would grow up to be soldiers but that is what every country boy believes. Dan and I broke in our new camouflage and I heard gravel popping from the road leading to our house. Dan and I snuck up the creek and hid in the bushes near the bridge. As the sound of gravel popping became louder I saw it was my dad coming home from work. My dad and Dan's dad both worked at the same rock quarry located about 25 miles from our home. My dad's left arm was hanging out the window of his non-air-conditioned truck. His face was dirty from all the dust in the rock quarry and his shirt was even dirtier. Dan and I remained concealed in the bushes until he went up the hill to our house. Dan and I went back to our training ground and in a few minutes I heard my Dad start up the tractor.

In April 2001, I was 33 years old. I wanted to live my country boy dream of being a Marine. I felt I had an obligation to serve my country, so I joined the Marine Corps Reserve. I left behind a wife, a job, and a home, so that for three months I could be trained to be a worthy member of the US Marine Corps. The war started in September 2001 when America was attacked.

I told my parents that I was being sent away for three months to do some training for my job as a federal agent. I lied to them because I felt they, like so many others, would not understand why I felt it was so important for me to live out this dream. As the bus stopped in front of a building, a tall, lean Marine drill instructor boarded the bus. He was dressed in well-pressed camouflage uniform. Attached to his waist was a green belt like the one I had growing up, but it had a shiny brass Marine Corps seal on it. His voice echoed through the bus and no one could move fast enough for him, not even the 19-year-old kids. He walked past me and I made eye contact with him. Clearly, that was a mistake. He turned and started to scream in my face for looking at him. I looked straight ahead but he continued to scream at me. I prayed he would move on. It felt like all the times I was in the woods trying to kill a turkey and a mosquito was trying to bite me. I knew if I moved the old turkey would see me but the mosquito would not go away. Unlike the mosquito, the drill instructor found more suitable prey and moved on to torment someone else. As he screamed at the young kid in front of me I felt bad for him but I was sure glad he had moved on.

If I had to recall my first week on Parris Island I doubt I could. I remember filling out paperwork, taking physical tests and being shuffled around like cattle from one building to the next. We were all fitted for the clothes that we would wear for the next three months. We received our camouflage pants and jackets and our names did not appear on them, and unlike the clothes from the surplus store these smelled brand new. We all wore the same clothes, shoes, hats, and received the standard Marine Corps haircut. I remember my first haircut on the island and how I wished it was my wife cutting my hair as she did every Sunday night until then. As the barber shaved my head his clippers felt like a chainsaw against my scalp. I must admit, the first week on the island I really regretted my decision to go there. I was turned down by several recruiters and was told it was because I was too old. I finally found a recruiter who could see the passion in my eyes to live out a childhood dream and he helped me find the road to Parris Island.

At the end of the first week we carried our gear to our new home. As we walked into the squad bay I recalled my father once said, "Everyone needs a place to call home." I watched the faces of the young kids as we walked into our new home and the fear in their faces will stay forever etched in my memory. The first person we met was our senior drill instructor. He was younger than me, had several tattoos and seemed to be well seasoned for a young man. I figured out right away that he was our friend and he was the first person on the island that actually talked to us. He presented himself as a father figure and I could tell that most of these kids needed one. He introduced his two right hand men, who were also drill instructors. He told us that one would teach us the skilled art that all Marines learn: drill. I did not understand the term drill but soon realized it meant being able to march. The other drill instructor would teach us the history of the Marine Corps.

Sister Mary, the Baker, the Barber, and the Bricklayer

The senior drill instructor had an office located on the squad bay floor. His office was also a room where every night one of our drill instructors would sleep. After the senior drill instructor finished laying down the ground rules he walked into his office and closed the door. As his door slammed it reminded me of interviewing prisoners in jail and hearing the slamming of the steel doors. The slamming door echoed down the concrete squad bay floor and then the right hand men turned into the hounds of hell and unleashed their wrath on us. The young kids scurried to find their place and the drill instructors screamed commands. I felt bad for the kids because they did not understand what was going on. I had never been in war but I had been in situations that went from calm to chaotic. That is what the drill instructors were doing. Our training had begun.

We were assigned a bed, which was referred to as a "rack." I chose the top rack and my young 18-year-old rack mate from New York took the bottom. As the chaos continued, I managed to make my rack. My rack reminded me of the bed my father made for my brother and me growing up. Someone he knew was getting new kitchen cabinets so my dad made captain's beds out of old kitchen cabinets and other wood. The beds were really tall and looked professionally made. My father was very good with his hands and could do almost anything. As we settled in, an occasional drill instructor would come by and torment us. Our platoon consisted of about 64 recruits. Since there were only two drill instructors one could have an occasional moment of peace.

On our first night in the squad bay I could hear some of the kids crying in their racks. I wanted to help them but I knew this was all part of the boot camp process. Some of these kids failed to realize that they had joined an organization that is training people for war. Prior to boot camp I had been through five separate law enforcement academies, but none of them prepared me for war. There is a lot of difference between being a police officer and being a Marine. As I tried to drift off to sleep, the one-room squad bay brought back memories of the fishing cabin that our family had growing up. Our cabin was one-room with cold running water and an outhouse. It wasn't much to look at but we spent every summer vacation and many weekends there. It was located on an unpopulated river about 100 miles from our home. As the kids cried I tried to concentrate on those nights at our cabin when the bullfrogs sang us to sleep.

Our first morning at the squad bay was like most mornings on Parris Island, early. I could tell that some of these kids never had to get up early in their lives. We had to clean the squad bay, clean the head (bathroom) and then it was off to chow (breakfast). The chow hall was not like any cafeteria I had ever eaten in. Recruits who had been on the island longer were the ones who served the food and drill instructors hovered over us like buzzards looking for prey. There was no talking between recruits and the food portions were small and the time to eat was very short. My best friend Dan grew up in a large family and one learned to eat very fast at his family table. As I shoveled as much food as I could get in my mouth I thought of how Dan always made fun of me because it took me so long to eat. We even had to drill when we moved about in the chow hall.

Everything on Parris Island is done for a reason. I think being older helped me see the reason and understand why we were told to do some of the things that seemed to make no sense. Boot camp is designed for the average recruit and the average recruit is usually overweight and not in shape. I learned the importance of being in shape and eating right from my father, so I was not an average recruit or an average 33-year-old man. I did not need to lose weight but with the small portions of food I soon realized I would be hungry as long as I was on this island.

The only day that recruits were given an option was Sunday. After morning chow a recruit could stay in the squad bay and write letters to home, polish his boots, or go to church. The option time frame was about four hours and after that it was back on. The first couple of Sundays I went to church because I felt I made a great mistake. I was on an island surrounded by kids who wanted to prove something to someone back home. Here I was a college-educated man with a wife, career, home and I just wanted to be a Marine. I would hear the kids talk about how they wanted to show their father, mother, brother, or guys back on the block that they could make it through boot camp. There were a few in my platoon that could have gone on to college after high school and been anything they wanted to be but they were like me, they wanted to be a Marine.

Boot camp was proof that, in our society, the military does not attract the best recruits. One could understand with the risks, low pay, and lack of patriotism in our kids today that most of them would prefer to go to college. I saw the same thing in my law enforcement field; that most kids today say that the risk of getting killed is not worth the money one is paid. When I graduated from high school I wanted to join the military but my father wanted me to go to college. He served in the Navy and after four years was discharged and went to work at the rock quarry. He always told me to that he wanted me to go to college so I could choose my career and be happy every day I went to work, and not be like him.

As I sat in the Catholic Church on Parris Island and listened to the priest preach his sermon, I thought about my father's words. I sat there a million miles from that island in my mind and a recruit who was returning from communion stopped and handed me his rosary. I turned to see if I knew him but I could tell by the wear on his camouflage clothing that he had been on the island much longer than me. You could always tell the new recruits by the smell of their new clothes or the lack of wear on them. As you progressed through the three phases of boot camp, each phase allowed you to wear your uniform more like a Marine versus a recruit. At the end of the final phase and if you passed all your tests you would receive your nametags, which were placed on your camouflage clothing. As the recruit walked through the church and returned to his seat I examined the rosary and placed it in my pocket. After that day in church I figured God was trying to send me a sign. I had attended a Catholic grade school and high school, and was even married in the Catholic Church but I did not consider myself a good Catholic. We were not allowed to have anything in our pockets, but I carried that rosary with me every day that I was on that island.

I went to church for a couple of Sundays then I started staying in the squad bay and writing letters to my wife and friends. I missed talking to someone who knew about paying taxes and having responsibilities. I would sit on my footlocker and write my letters but the complaints from the kids on how they missed fast food, their car, and video games would sometimes filter between my thoughts and the paper I was writing on. As I wrote letters during those four hours of peace, I struggled with the lie I had told my parents. In 1997, my father had a malignant tumor removed from his lower back. A year later another malignant tumor grew back in the same spot but this time the surgery left him without the use of one of his legs and several other complications. One Sunday I finally decided to write my father a letter and tell him that I was not away on some job-related training but was a recruit on Parris Island. A part of me did not want to tell him the truth because I knew he would want to attend my graduation. I knew the trip from his house to the island would be very hard with all his health problems.

Our platoon came together like an automobile being built in a factory, and I could see the confidence being built in each recruit. The recruits that were out of shape were losing weight and becoming both physically and mentally stronger. I had surgery on my left elbow about a year and half before boot camp and it started to cause me some pain about a month into boot camp. I had reported the surgery to the Marine Corps when I joined up and I thought it would not cause me any problems but I guess the everyday physical training was too much. I never said a word to any of the drill instructors because I did not want to be sent to a platoon behind me while my elbow healed. At night we would bring an ice chest from the chow hall and after lights were out I would ice my elbow. My favorite part of boot camp was when we would go for a run as a platoon. The drill instructor would yell out cadence and we would respond. We would run through the pine trees and sandy soil of South Carolina yelling back to the drill instructor. I would look down at my sweatshirt and on my left breast was the eagle, globe and anchor, the symbol of the Marine Corps. My shoes hitting the sandy soil brought back the days of running the gravel roads with my best friend Dan as we were headed to our secret training ground. I would break out in goose bumps thinking about my dream coming true.

Every evening was mail call. The senior drill instructor would have recruits stack up three footlockers and he would use them as a desk and pass out the mail. I learned to love mail call, as did most recruits. I loved getting letters from people back home who were my age and older. It was nice to hear from people who did not miss fast food.

My father never did write me but my wife wrote me a letter and said she spoke to him and he did receive his letter. The senior drill instructor would use this time to also answer questions from recruits. I found this time to be a little strange and I assumed that twenty years ago it never would have happened on the island. In the last twenty years the island has been under attack from the peering eyes of the American society who sometimes disagree with some of the island's training tactics. One time after mail call a recruit in my platoon complained to the senior drill instructor that one of our drill instructors spoke rough to him. I was so outraged that I asked permission to speak to the platoon. The senior drill instructor granted me permission and I told the recruits that this was not Boy Scout camp and these men were teaching us how to stay alive in combat. I continued to tell them, "If speaking rough to you upsets you, what will you do when your best friend next to you is blown up in combat?" I said a lot more, but soon realized some of these kids still did not get the purpose of what these men were preparing them for. One of my best friends who had been through boot camp 13 years prior to me told me before I left, "Boot camp was for a certain person at a certain time in their life." As I laid my head down to sleep that night I realized I was that person but my timing was off.

My frustration with the kids only got worse every day. I observed several kids turn around and become part of the platoon. I also observed several kids who realized we were more than halfway through boot camp and saw no reason to change now. I know from talking to Marines that twenty years ago recruits who did not want to accept the Marine Corps way of life would have been

46

given extra physical training but some people in our society believe that boot camp should be easy. Boot camp is training that prepares one for war and war has never been easy. I could see the frustration on the drill instructors' faces as they tried to be a father, peer, role model, and disciplinarian to these kids. I gathered from the conversations I overheard on my Sunday mornings that most of these kids came from broken homes and desperately needed some type of role model. The drill instructors would have to walk a thin line to train "America's Play Station generation" in what seemed like a long three months but in reality the time was not long enough.

Observing the training at boot camp reminded me of training dogs. I had been involved in training German Shepherds as a hobby for over seven years. The training that I was involved with consisted of three parts: obedience, protection, and tracking. I would never put a lot of pressure on a puppy but when a dog reached a year of age the training would begin. I saw the recruits as just reaching a year old and now it was time for their training to begin. The average age on Parris Island was 19 and most of the kids in my platoon were around that age. In dog training I would push a dog until I would almost break them but back off so they leave the training field with confidence. I would teach the dogs that if they do what I say they would be rewarded. I saw a lot of similarities between the drill instructors and myself when it came to training. The recruits had to be taught discipline and how to follow orders. The recruits also had to be taught how to survive in combat, fire a weapon, and be proficient in hand-to-hand combat. Some of these kids had never even held a weapon; let alone fire one. By the time you leave Parris Island you will be able to fire a M-16 rifle with iron sights from 500 yards and hit the target. How the drill instructors are able to accomplish that feat still amazes me to this day.

By the third month I could see that I was getting closer to making my dream a reality. Our training now was more focused on preparing the recruits for combat. I recall one night when we moved through the woods in broken down groups from our platoon. The training was designed to simulate an active combat zone. The drill instructors had placed booby traps that if tripped by a recruit it would set off a loud firecracker. The drill instructors would also set off flares in the air to light up the woods so the recruits would learn not to move when the woods were lit up.

I do not think most of the recruits cared for me because I wasn't very understanding about all their complaints. I did not need positive reinforcement at the end of the day to encourage me to do better the next day. All I wanted was to be able to walk across that parade deck on graduation day and be a Marine. As we moved through the woods I found a trip wire attached to the large firecracker. I told the recruits with me and directed them to crawl around it. I started to disarm the booby trap but soon realized the recruits that followed would not learn anything. I started to crawl forward deeper into the woods and on my boot heals were several recruits who decided at that particular moment they liked me. I learned about booby traps from looking for marijuana fields as a police officer. I also knew about booby traps from my adventures with Dan growing up as we trained for all the wars we would fight when we became soldiers. My elbow was not too fond of the pressure that was placed on it as we crawled. I was attempting to crawl a little higher off the ground to take some of the pressure off my elbow when out of the shadows a drill instructor put his foot on my Kevlar helmet and drove my face in the mud. He yelled, "Keep your head down or it will get shot off." I didn't say a word and continued to crawl through the woods. A recruit knew from day one on Parris Island to never make eye contact with a drill instructor and to answer all questions or commands with "yes sir, no sir," and "aye, sir." I figured if I kept my head down and kept crawling I should be ok with not saying anything.

One day one of the drill instructors from my platoon grabbed me and instructed me to come with him. As I followed him to the truck he never said a word and it was not permitted for me to talk to him. I climbed in the back of the truck because recruits were not allowed to ride in the front. We bounced along the roads of the island and I could not help but think about the day Dan and I went to the surplus store. Because the island relies on recruits for everything I felt confident I was grabbed to do some work. As recruits get close to graduation every platoon has one week of being assigned to maintenance or chow hall duty. My platoon was assigned to maintenance and my specific duty was to paint the squad bay. As we rode through the island I wondered where we were going but I dared not ask. The drill instructor parked at some building and I was instructed to follow him into the building. As we entered the building I saw a large pile of brand new camouflage clothes. The drill instructor told me to load the clothes into the back of the truck. As I loaded the clothes I saw that they had the names above the pockets and the names were kids from my platoon. I waited since I was a kid to see my name above the pockets of a camouflage jacket but I did not see my name in the piles. As we returned to the squad I was told by the drill instructor to sort the camouflage clothes out and place them on the appropriate recruits rack. After several piles I finally found my name above the pocket and on the other pocket it said "U.S. Marine Corps." I smiled deep inside and wished that Dan could see me now. When the recruits returned to the squad bay the excitement was in the air when they saw their name in print and they knew that graduation was just around the corner. That same evening the senior drill instructor passed out our dog tags. We were instructed to put them in our footlockers until we were told to wear them. All the kids were real excited to get their dog tags but I wasn't. Dan and I never cared much for dog tags because we associated dog tags with being a way to identify those killed in combat.

The final obstacle to graduating or escaping the island is the "Crucible." The "Crucible" is several days of little sleep, little food, plenty of exercising, and lots of teamwork. Our platoon was broken down into groups and each one of our drill instructors was assigned to a group. My group consisted of a lot of the kids who were trying to slip through boot camp. The drill instructor that was assigned to my group was the senior drill instructor. Over the next few days we would work as a team and see if we learned anything in the last three months. I was frustrated more than once with the kids in my group but we managed to complete the "Crucible."

Sister Mary, the Baker, the Barber, and the Bricklayer

We left the field early one morning and marched back to the squad bay. My backpack was heavy but I knew now that I had become a Marine. We stopped at the chow hall and for the first time on the island I left the chow hall feeling full.

The next morning we were instructed to wear our camouflage that had our names on it. As I slipped my jacket on I smelled the new smell that reminded me of my first days on the island. My name above my pocket looked a lot better than the magic marker I wore as a kid. We were told from now until we graduated we would wear our new camouflage but we were still not Marines.

The day before graduation family and friends are allowed to come to the island and visit for about four hours in the afternoon. As I put on my uniform I was really nervous to see my wife and friends. I knew it was stupid to be nervous but I had not seen my wife in three months. As we marched over to the parade deck where our family and friends waited in the bleachers, I saw my wife. Her hair glowed in the sunny South Carolina sky and tears rolled from my eyes. It was hard not to cry because for three months we had been trained not to show emotions of any kind and I had a lot built up. The drill instructor released us and like dogs running to catch a ball, we embraced our family and friends. I never thought a hug from my wife could feel so good. We were allowed to take our family and friends around the island and show them where we had spent the last three months. One of my friends who graduated from Parris Island 13 years ago came along with my wife. My mother- and father-in-law were also there. Those four hours seemed like two minutes and it was back to the squad bay.

Almost every night after the lights went out the drill instructor that was on duty would walk up and down the squad bay and talk to the recruits. Most of the time what he would say reminded me of what my father would say to me before I went to bed. Bedtime was of the very few times that one could hear compassion in the voice of a drill instructor. Our last night on the island the senior drill instructor told us, "America does not need a Marine Corps but they want one." He continued to say, "The Marine Corps is

America's 911 force." As the sound of his boots could be heard walking up and down the squad bay he cited years and years of history where the Marines have been the first ones in and sometimes the last ones out. The last words the senior drill instructor said to us that night before he closed his door was, "Greatness, no matter how brief, stays with a man forever." In my 33 years of living the best sleep I ever had was on Parris Island, which seems strange to most people. I had absolutely no control over anything and no responsibilities. My job for three months was to wake up and give my all. That last night on Parris Island was a long one. I tried to sleep but I knew the next day my dream would come true.

My platoon and I marched onto the parade deck with five other platoons graduating that day. I was told that, out of the 352 graduating that day, I was the oldest by far.

As my dress uniform shoes struck the pavement we marched in front of the bleachers. I tried my best to fight the tears but it was useless. I thought of my father and how he had served his country in the Navy. I also thought of my Catholic Priest and how he had served his country in the Marine Corps before he became a priest. I thought about my best friend who was also the best man in my wedding and how he served his country in the Marine Corps. I stood there with tears rolling down my face thinking about these men who I felt were responsible for me making it this far. I looked up and saw the American flag flying in the South Carolina sky and thought of all the Marines from World War One to Desert Storm who have stood on this hallowed ground. I felt the goose bumps rise from my arms and realized at that moment that our flag became more than a piece of cloth, or a reason to get up out of my school seat, it became a part of me. I never really felt a part of anything growing up but as the Marine Corps Marching Band played and our flag whipped in the wind, I felt honored and special to stand on an island that some referred to as hell. I looked up and the drill instructor stood in front of me and handed me my eagle, globe, and anchor. I was now officially a Marine. I held the pin in my hand and wondered if Dan could feel the joy in my heart.

Sister Mary, the Baker, the Barber, and the Bricklayer

The drill instructor released us from formation and I searched for my family and friends. It was then that I realized I was no different than the kids I'd spent the last three months with. I looked for my father in hope that he had come but I never saw him. I stood there in confusion at all the people and knew my father would have trouble getting onto the parade deck. I continued to look for a handicapped man but he was not there. I guess no matter how old you are if you love your father you still want his approval. Before I could have another thought about my father, my wife was hugging me. Once again her hug never felt so good.

Through my tears I saw my best man, which was a big surprise. I hugged him and more tears fell from my face. When I moved away from home my best man taught me the world of law enforcement. In many ways he was a second father to me. He once gave me a book titled "From Father To Son." He wrote these words on the inside cover, "I'm not trying to compete with your dad, in fact some of the quotes sound like something your dad would write. Share them with him! Pass it on to your child. Keep life simple even after you rise to the top." I then looked up to see my boss, two coworkers, and several more friends had shown up. As we made our way to the parking lot, my best man handed me a gift. It was a wooden plaque that he got when he was in the Marine Corps. The plaque said, "For those who must fight for it, life has a special flavor the protected never know." We all said our goodbyes and headed home. As we crossed the bridge leaving Parris Island my wife handed me my father's Navy bracelet. My father gave it to me when I was a little boy. On one side has his name and on the other side it says US Navy and has his service number. I wear it every day.

A few weeks after boot camp my friend who had graduated from Parris Island 13 years ago came to visit. My friend asked me how my elbow was. I had not told anybody that my elbow still bothered me even though I had not done any pull-ups in weeks. I told my friend that it hurt a lot in boot camp and still hurts today. He said I should report it to my reserve unit before it was injured worse. I reported it to my reserve unit on my next reserve drill. I was put on light duty and told to see my family doctor. I went to my doctor and he prescribed anti-inflammatory medication and therapy. He said to come back in a month. I returned to my doctor to have my elbow examined once again. It appeared the medication had not helped and my condition was the same. My doctor had to report his findings to my reserve unit every month. I knew if my elbow did not get better in six months I would be medically discharged.

Two months after boot camp I returned to the woods where Dan and I grew up. Every Spring I return so Dan and I can go turkey hunting. As Dan and I looked out over the morning fog I briefly returned in my mind to one of the many early mornings on Parris Island. As we listened for a gobbler, I smiled when I looked inside my camouflage jacket and saw my Marine Corps sweatshirt. I could not help but wonder where I would be now if I had gone to boot camp at 18. I guess I'll never know the answer to that question but I'm glad I had the chance to go at 33. Dan and I spent the next week together and I told him all about those three months on Parris Island. Dan worked at a rock quarry and was a farmer on the side. He was married and had two kids. As our week of being kids again came to an end I drove away from Dan's house headed back to the place I call home. In my rear view mirror I could see the bumper sticker on the back of Dan's old four-wheel drive truck. The sticker said "Marines."

I was glad to be back at work and the adjustment from Parris Island to the civilian world was not as easy as I thought. I found a need to spend more time in the woods than I had in past years. I was deer hunting on some property that I was not familiar with and I snuck up on a buck and I took a shot at him. I hit the buck but he ran off. I tracked him for a while but it had been raining for days and it was hard to find the blood trail. I went back to my truck and took one of my German Shepherds with me. I had trained my dogs to track people, and I also trained them to track a wounded deer. As my dog trailed the deer we ended up about a mile from where I had shot it. The deer was not bleeding very much, so I felt my shot might not have been a good one. My dog trailed the deer to a creek that was flowing pretty swiftly. It

53

appeared the deer had swum the creek. I stepped into the edge of the creek to see how deep it was and the swift waters grabbed me and filled up my rubber boots. I was sucked under by the current and pulled down the stream. As I fought to swim to the top of the water I struggled to get to the bank. I finally made it to the bank and grabbed a branch and pulled myself out. I was greeted by the wet kisses of my dog. The water was cold and I was now even colder. As the cold water ran down my back, I lay on the bank and thanked God that I did not drown. My dog went back to the end of the blood trail and sniffed the ground. I told her that we could not swim across that creek. She lay down and put both her paws in the edge of the water. I stood there and recalled the pool on Parris Island and how we were trained to swim with full combat gear on including a rifle. I told my dog to stay and I tightened up my belt and jumped in. I swam across the creek and I ended up about 20 yards down the creek. I crawled up the bank and called my dog to me. She jumped in and I followed her down the creek and helped her get out. We continued to track the deer but the trail was getting hard to follow. I knew now we were a good mile and half from my truck. It would be dark in an hour and if we did find the deer I wondered how we would get him across the creek. I kneeled down to my dog and told her it was time to go home. It was a hard decision because you always want to leave the training field with confidence that you accomplished the mission. My dog felt we had failed but I knew my training had paid off, maybe not in combat but in my everyday life. We returned to the creek and swam back across.

My unit went to war in Iraq, but I received a medical discharge because of my elbow. I knew then that it was final and had to accept the fact that I was no longer in the Marine Corps. Many people tried to make me feel better about it by saying I was already serving my country in my current job but I still felt my dream was short lived. A few months went by and I packed up most of my Marine Corps clothing and gave it to a friend of mine whose grandson is serving in Iraq.

A few months ago my wife and I and our friend who graduated from Parris Island 13 years ago took a trip. We went to many places but the place I really wanted to see was the place where the movie "Field of Dreams" was filmed. The movie has been an inspiration to me more than once to follow my dreams no matter how crazy people think I was. I looked over the ball field and cornfield and thought about all the people who said I was crazy for joining the Marine Corps. I thought about all the dreams I had and how glad I was that I pursued the Marine Corps one, even though it did not turn out the way I wanted. I watched the kids play in the ball field and hope they too will believe in their dreams and follow their heart.

It's late as I type these final words about the long road to Parris Island. I'm in the room that my wife refers to as my room. I think about Parris Island often. Many people have asked me what makes Marines so special. I tell them that what I did on the island was fundamentally what Marines were doing 50 years ago. Parris Island is in the business of turning boys into men who will survive horrific situations. Parris Island is not a boy-scout camp. The training there helps one to leave the training field confident. As I reflect on those days, I look up at the wall in front of me and there hangs the plaque given to me by my friend. Hanging on one corner of the plaque are my dog tags that have never been worn and hanging on the other corner of the plaque is the rosary. Hanging on the back of an old wooden chair is one of my camouflage jackets with my name above one pocket and the US Marine Corps above the other pocket and the jacket still smells like a new recruit. On one of the walls are several pictures of my friends and family on graduation day. There is also a picture of me with the recruiter who believed in me. On a shelf sits an old green belt from the days when Dan and I were training to be soldiers. I sit in this room often and reflect on days gone by. I have many things in this room to remind me of who I am, where I have been, and where I would like to go. My time on Parris Island provided me with the opportunity to re-examine who I am. I first thought I was much different than the recruits who wanted to prove something to somebody but in the end I realized I was no different.

My father had come to realize his own mortality and he told me how he wished he had been a better father. I've concluded that fathers will always think they could have done more and sons will always look for their father's approval no matter how old they are. I went to college like my father wanted but I don't always like my job or feel satisfied with it. If I pick up a hammer and build something with my hands and have sweat roll down my back I feel I've done something. At the end of a day when I've used a shovel and my hands are calloused from hard work, I walk away dirty but I feel good and confident. Even though I did what my father asked and went to college I sometimes think I'd been better off in the rock quarry. In the back of a closet is one Marine Corps uniform that I kept. When the good Lord felt my father could leave His training field confident, I wore that uniform when they laid his body to rest. As for his soul, it will always be with me when I sweat like he did, being my father's son.

Written to my father: the man he was, the man he had become, and the man that will be remembered.

- WLV-

Comments on Chapter 4

Types of Memory

The brain formulates several different types of memory. One is known as kinesthetic memory. All right, I can imagine some people just glazed over. Sorry, sometimes people with a Ph.D. just can't help themselves and we have to throw out a word like 'kinesthetic' every now and then. It simply means movement memory. If we did not have it, we would not remember how to walk when we got out of bed each day. We would not be able to move in a coordinated fashion and we would spend a lot of time with our faces against the ground. Once you learn to ride a bike, you have that memory tucked away in your brain permanently. If you haven't ridden a bike in a long time, you still have a memory of how it is done. The only problem is getting your out-of-shape muscles to cooperate with the memory.

Short Term Memory

The brain also has short-term memory and long-term memory. Short-term memories are useful in the here and now. For example, if you are in a strange town and you need to find an address, the directions, "At the second traffic light turn left onto Sherman Street and that building will be on your right" go into the short term memory system. They are useful for the moment. If you never plan to have to go to that address again, it doesn't matter if you brain forgets the address once you find it and complete your task. A few months ago, for instance, I had to go to a town in New Jersey where I had never been before to get a copy of the deed for my sister's house, which our family was selling. The GPS did not have enough information so I had to stop and get directions from a local person. I found the place I needed and completed my task. Today, I could not tell you now how to get there. Short-term memory is limited.

Long Term memory

Long-term memories are developed when we have repetition of the subject matter. There is old adage. "In repetition, there is learning." We repeat our ABC's again and again because they are the building blocks of words and we need words to communicate. We practice a football play over and over until we can execute without hesitation. We study a particular subject for a test multiple times before we are confident to take the test. Getting a memory into the long-term memory system also depends on sleep. So pulling an all-nighter and taking a test without sleep is not as effective in learning as studying in several bursts and then sleeping and then covering the material again before taking the test. (I hope some of my university students read this!)

Eye-Hand-Skill Coordination

The brain sometimes has to combine different types of memories. To learn an eye-hand-skill coordination function, it normally takes at least five exposures to the experience with some practice before we get it down pretty well. The brain will need to combine short- term, long-term, and kinesthetic (there it is again) memories to learn a skill that requires the use of eyes, hands, body posture, and technical memories. Learning to shoot at a target is a perfect example of learning eye-hand-skill coordination functions.

The Emergency Memory System

The brain also has an emergency memory system. The emergency memory system cannot wait out five exposures to a life-threatening stimulus before the brain gets the message. If we had to experience a dangerous event five times before we figured out that it could kill us, we would have a high potential of dying before we learned the lesson. In the emergency memory system, the brain perceives the threat, attaches a strong emotional component, like fear, and then generates intense, immediate, and permanent memories. One exposure to a terrifying event is sufficient for the development of the emergency memory. The emergency memory, of course, should steer us away from future threatening events. If not, then we will make Darwin look like a genius and we won't be around to argue the point.

Associated Memories

There are other memory systems in the brain. For instance, there are **associated memories** and **dissociated memories**. Associated memories are the normal healthy ones. The disassociated memories are a bit of a problem if we don't understand them and know how to control and work with them.

The story, "My Father's Son," is a perfect example of a healthy form of memory called **Associated Memories**. Josey remembers boyhood memories of his friend Dan and going to the army surplus store to get military clothing. He remembers his Marine Corps training at Parris Island. He remembers what people said and did there and what it was like to graduate. He remembers how to swim fully dressed with a full pack because the Marine Corps taught him that and he had to practice it several times. That long-term memory saved his life when he got caught in a strongly flowing stream. The story is filled with associated memories.

Associated Memories have the following characteristics:

- They are normal long-term memories
- Each memory is distinct and separated from each other, but they are associated (linked) with other memories
- Memories can be mentally filed in a chronological order. The memories Josey brings up in the story are chronological in order
- One memory can inform other memories
- The memories hang together smoothly
- A full memory of an experience is formed.
- Bad memories (being swept downstream) are tempered by good memories (being licked by his dog).

- We can direct our memories to solve problems and to formulate innovations. (He wrote a letter to his Dad admitting that he had joined the Marine Corps).
- Memories are stored in the context in which they occurred like files in a file cabinet. (He could tell the whole story or just focus on one part of the story. Each part of a story could be expanded out into it's own separate story.)
- The Hippocampus and prefrontal cortex are calm. (Whoa! Here we go again with the big words. Steady, partner, all that simply means is that the emotions and thoughts are in concert [harmony] with the memories. There are no obsessive thoughts and no extreme emotions. All is good with the world.)
- Each memory is stored in context with appropriate emotions attached. It's cool!
- Each memory has a beginning and an ending
- We can direct our thinking into pleasant memories or choose unpleasant memories without losing control
- We can shut off or switch memories at will
- We will cover the dissociated memories in the Chapter 5 comments section. Getting the associated memories clear is enough for now. See the diagram of associated memories below. It may help to clarify the concept of associated memories

Associated Memories

Each ball represents a memory element (the five senses, emotions, thoughts, body sensations, situations, circumstances, and threats). The funnel represents the brain, which processes and connects the memory elements. Once the brain processes the memory elements there is a sense of completeness and wholeness.

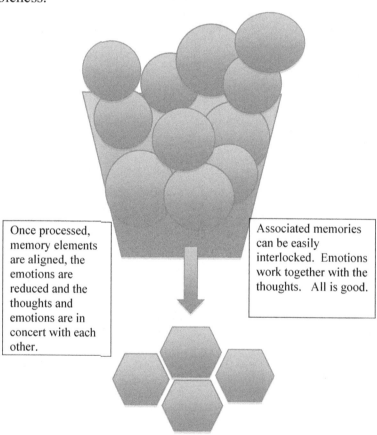

Once processed, memory elements are aligned, the emotions are reduced and the thoughts and emotions are in concert with each other.

Associated memories can be easily interlocked. Emotions work together with the thoughts. All is good.

- JTM -

61

CHAPTER 5

The Door Holder

My father handed me the other end of the board as we were building the carport behind our house. I held the board up and told him the board was not straight. He said, "Get it as close as you can and hammer a nail in it because some boards will never be straight." I hammered the nail into the board and looked over to my father as he smiled in approval.

I was around 18 years old when I helped my father build that carport. Over the years I had learned how to be a carpenter, a plumber, an electrician, a gardener, and a mechanic from my father. He took great pride in fixing things and seldom did he have anyone build or fix anything for us. My father was a man of few words, but when he spoke, I knew to listen.

I stood before a group of men and women who had decided to learn how to become peer responders; a job that simply means coming to the aid of others who have been in an event that was too hard to process. Peer responders attempt to build those people back up, after their world was torn down around them. Peer support is an attempt to fix their broken pieces.

As I spoke to the class over the next several days, my mind drifted back to our small farm where it all started for me, and the many times my father would say, "Now pay attention to what I'm fixin' to show you because one day I will not be around." I have learned over the years that those in front of me might want to assist others through an event, or maybe deep down inside they are seeking how to process that one event that is stuck in their own mind, and sometimes in their soul. In this particular class, one man stands out, maybe because his hair looks like John

Travolta from Saturday Night Fever or maybe because he has a look of pain. In my head I named him the Redneck John Travolta. I learned that look of pain after my father went through his first bout with cancer, but since that time I have also learned that people can have a look of emotional pain.

As I continued to wear a path in the carpet, all I could do was focus on the Redneck John Travolta. He was a polished speaker and when he spoke in class he had everyone on the edge of their seats. He made a joke, as most fire fighters do, and then spoke of a fatal fire from 10 years ago. He told the class he had never talked about the fire, but he gave us a brief view of a fire where three kids had died and how he broke all of the fire fighter rules trying to save them.

After class that day, I struggled to sleep because I had put my heart and soul into teaching. I tried to convey to those in front of me the purpose of peer work. Most think it's to make others feel better, but in reality our job is to help those who have been traumatized to process the event, and for a brief moment, give them a break from it. I often think peer support work is more like holding a door open for someone, giving him or her a brief break from the path they are on. I was unable to do that from my worn path in the classroom for the Redneck John Travolta.

On day two, I told the class of a story where a fire investigator was troubled by a fire he was investigating. The whole family had died and all that survived was a rabbit on the back porch. The fire had singed the hair on the rabbit, but it was still alive. I had no answer as to why the rabbit survived and why the family died. As a peer responder it's a very helpless feeling when you cannot provide some relief to those in front of you. I compare it to when your child wakes up with an earache and all you can do is hold them until the doctor's office opens. I had no answer for the fire investigator, so weeks later I mailed him a small plastic rabbit and simply said, "many times in life we are the rabbit." As I told this story to the class I walked back to the Redneck John Travolta and handed him a small plastic rabbit. He smiled, and with watered eyes, made a joke.

The next day, the Redneck John Travolta sat in front of the class and me and told a story that he had kept buried for 10 years. He was committed to saving the kids and said he would have died trying. He rescued the kids from the house, but it was too late. When I asked, "Why are you talking about it now?" He answered, "It was time."

The next week, I loaded up my boys and drove to my home state to spend some time with my mom. As my mom did what grandma's do, I sat in the wooden swing that is under the carport that my father and I built some 30 years ago. I looked at the house and all of the out buildings my father had built. I saw the detail in the carpentry, plumbing, and electrical work that he did. On a wall in the house is a piece of wood that dad handed to me the last time we cut firewood. I cleaned it up and mounted it to a board. My dad enjoyed cutting wood, but when dad handed it to me he was recovering from his first bout with cancer, and he was in a lot of physical pain. As he handed the piece of wood to me he said, "I'm done and I cannot do this anymore." Years later, he took basket weaving classes and became a very good basket weaver. At that moment, his obsession with cutting firewood and basket weaving became clear to me; it made him feel emotionally better. My wife once told me a quote by Mary Reilly who was an Occupational Therapist. She said, "Man, through the use of his hands, as they are energized by mind and will, can influence the state of his own health." My father found peace from the emotional and physical tolls of cancer by cutting wood and basket weaving.

On that visit to my home state, my mom complained of her knee that was injured by a horse some 60 years ago, but she said she had learned to live with it. She said, "It's hard sometimes, living in the house your father built. Everywhere I look, there is something he made or fixed. I stay here because the longer I stay here, the more it brings me comfort from him being gone."

The next leg of our journey was to drive half way across the United States to meet a first responder and take him to the nonprofit site where I do volunteer work. My mom said that she would like to go on the ride and after a week she would fly back home. Along our route we stopped to visit an old friend of mine. I named him Crazy Bill years ago. As we sat on his back porch, and my boys fished in his pond in front of us, he told my mom and me how his girlfriend of ten years had cheated on him with another man, and then left him. His barrel chest, big arms and loud voice all seemed so small when he spoke of his pain. I searched for an answer as my mom looked at me as the expert in this area. I simply asked, "What has been the happiest time in your life?" He said, "The ten years with her." I said, "People spend all kinds of money on pills and material objects to be happy, so I think you were lucky to find someone who could make you happy. Life does not always work out like we want it to, but you had ten years of happiness with her and no one can take that from you." He looked at me, smiled, and said, "I never thought about it that way." As we drove from his house, my mom bragged on me for my response, and I said, "It was timing mom, he was ready for an answer."

As we pulled up to the airport curb, there stood the first responder I had met a few weeks ago. In my head I had named him Batman. He stood there, broken down and scared. My mom and boys made this trip to distract him from what it was really about, which was trying to save him from the images that had gotten inside of his head.

Many years ago he had worked a bad scene and a few weeks ago, while sitting in one of my classes, the bad scene was stirred back up in him and now he was seeking some relief from those images. My boys knew this Batman was not as brave and strong as the one in the movies, but they did their best to take his mind off of why he was there. While I checked Batman into the nonprofit site, which is nothing more than a two-story farmhouse tucked away on 29 acres, my boys fed apples and carrots to the donkeys. My mom sat on the back porch and as a natural care giver, she attempted to bring peace to all those around her. The next few days were hard on Batman as he tried to unfold the layers of horror that had now become his life. Before that, the bad scene only seemed to be dream.

One night, we were gathered around a campfire at the nonprofit, and my oldest son was showing some of the first responders his flashlight, but one man just stared into the fire as if my son was not even there. As we drove back to the hotel, my oldest son said, "Daddy what was wrong with that man looking into the fire?" I said, "He is really sad." My son said, "Why is the man so sad?" I said, "Most of us in this business want to protect and shelter the people of the world from bad things and when kids die or get hurt it makes us sad, we feel like we failed at our job." My son asked, "Why do kids dying make them sadder than adults dying?" I said, "Because kids don't know much about the world. Kids are innocent and have not really lived life." My son said, "Daddy it's ok, I have a lot of the world in me." I had no comment to his answer and fought back the tears. My son said, "Daddy are you crying?" I said, "No, but if you don't quit, I will be."

After a week at the nonprofit, we took Batman back to the airport and he seemed better. He had a smile on his face and he learned that he was not alone in his battle to maintain the life he had before this job.

Our next stop was to visit an old friend who lives in a big city with tall buildings and lots of concrete. My boys were nervous as we drove by the tallest buildings they had ever seen, but I explained that in order to appreciate what you have, you have to see how the rest of the world lives. It had been many years since I had seen my friend and although he looked the same, he was tired. Years ago I had named him the Mastodon, but never told him that. By far, he is a breed of human that will one day be extinct. He has served the system well, but the system has not always served him well. He puts all others before his own health and life and my only hope is that, one day, I will be able to carry him to a place where he can finally get some rest. I have tried to get him to see the light, but all I can do is be his friend, which most of the time does not seem like enough. The Mastodon took me and my boys to a large concrete pond located amongst all of the tall buildings. My boys questioned what the pond was for so I kneeled down and explained that many years ago there were two large buildings here and some men, who did not like America, crashed planes into the buildings. And, as a result, many first responders and other people died here. My oldest son said, "I read about that in a book daddy." My youngest son looked at me like many people still look when they recall that day. As we walked the streets with my friend, I asked the Mastodon, "What do you do for yourself?" He smiled and said, "I don't know and I know that is not good." We hugged the Mastodon and I simply said, "I don't have time to come back up here and carry you so you better figure out how to take care of yourself." Sometimes even with a friend, all you can do is let them know you care.

A few days later, as we drove up to the gates, my youngest son said, "Daddy, I see the eagle, globe and anchor, where are we?" I said, "This is where daddy went to boot camp and I have not been back here since I graduated." As we drove around the base and saw the recruits in training, goose bumps covered my body. I love my family, but a part of me wanted to be a recruit again. I wanted to feel that feeling that only those who have been here can understand. I parked and said to the boys, "Let's walk down this street." My boys ran to the golden footprints painted on the street and said, "What are these for?" I said, "When you first come here, you have to stand on these prints and attempt to fill the shoes of all those before you. As you stand there, the largest, meanest, swamp mosquito flies around your head yelling at you and all you can do is stand there and listen." My boys found a set of footprints to stand on and as I looked at them, what was long overdue, burst out from under my sunglasses. My oldest son said, "Daddy are you crying?" I said, "Yes, I am this time." He asked, "Why?" I kneeled down and said, "When you grow up you will see things and have to do things that you cannot imagine. How you think life will turn out, seldom does, and many people will be hard on you for the wrong reasons. Your innocence will be stripped from you and on some days it's hard to be strong, I don't mean physically strong, but emotionally strong. I don't believe in magic, but what happens here, behind these gates, is magic. Besides your grandpa and others, when I was here, the magic to be strong was put in me, and no matter how hard the world or humans try, they cannot take it out of me, and that is why I'm crying. That feeling is so powerful, that I needed to know where it came from again." I'm not sure they understood what I said, but I know they felt it.

The next day, my wife greeted us as we drove into our driveway. After 28 days on the road and 6400 miles, we were home. My wife could tell I was tired, in many ways, and that I needed my woods to bring me peace. After a few days in the woods, I was on another plane heading to where a group of people wanted to hear what I have to say about peer support. To me, teaching is like going to the dentist. I dislike going, but I enjoy that my teeth are clean. As I taught this group, my mind drifted back to my dad and me building that carport. I looked at this group of people and saw that some were bent, broken, and most were in search of answers that, most of the time, I do not have. I tell them what I know and what I have seen, and some are able to feel what I have felt. A few days after the class, I got an email from a guy in the class who had clearly felt what I felt. He said, "After many years, someone finally gets it, thank you." He told me his story, which was a rough one, and I named him the Dirt Road Boy in my head. He explained that after the class was over he felt like a weight had been lifted off of his shoulders. I did not enjoy teaching the class, but I did enjoy his email.

It has been six months since that trip with my boys, and I sit here in the swamp some twenty feet off the ground. My seat is smaller than my butt and my feet rest on a platform about the size of a small car floor mat. Its deer season and my freezers are full, but I come here with all the pieces to the puzzle that I collect all year. Many times I see the job of peer support as like putting a puzzle together. We help them find the corner pieces and build from there. I come to this swamp to put the pieces of everyone I've met together. I need to know how everyone fits into my life. I feel blessed and privileged to have met you and to have maybe given you a break from the harsh realities of life.

It has now been over five years since I came down this path of peer support, and many have told me that I have a gift. It has taken years for me to accept my ability, but if you ask me, at times, it is a double-edged sword. I have been criticized for my out-of-the-box thinking in the way that I do peer support. I have been questioned on the fact that I appear to get too close to the people that I am trying to help. When I teach, or sit across from someone, I have one goal in mind; I want them to know that I care and no matter the time of day, I will be there for them. I have no idea what it is like to have someone die next to me, but I can relate to the loss of a loved one. There was also a time, years ago, when a question lived in my head, "Does anyone really care about me?" I know that the feeling that comes from this question is a horrible and isolated feeling. As such, I want everyone who hears my voice to feel all of my heart and know that I care. The double-edged sword is not the sad stories or the intense emotional pain that people share with me; I have no issues feeling that from you. It's being the guy at the front of the room. It's being the guy who is no longer anonymous when you do an Internet search. It's the guy who used to have his stories safely tucked away in a desk drawer, but now they are in a book for people to read. The double-edged sword is being criticized for pouring your heart out to those in front of you. The double-edged sword is being torn between the aggravation of all the administrative issues that surround the simple act of being able to sit knee cap to knee cap with a full grown man, who has a really bad earache, and the overwhelming satisfaction of helping someone put the pieces of their puzzle back together.

My Mom said the other day, "You will be famous one day." I know my Mom is proud as a parent. I get that now, but when I walk up in front of a class, my mind wanders back to the round oak table that sits in my parents' home. I can smell the toasted peanut butter and jelly sandwich that my mom would cook and I can hear her scraping the over toasted side off in the kitchen sink. In front of me is the small black and white television and playing is my favorite show growing up, "The Lone Ranger." I would eat my sandwich and dream of the people I would help when I grew up. As the morning air would hit my face, I would walk the dark quarter mile lane through the pine tree thicket to catch the school bus. As my shoes landed on the gravel, I would dream of the man I would be one day. I wrote a story years ago called "The Men Behind the Mask." It's about a time in my life where I did not wear a mask, but was a good guy pretending to be a bad guy. The story sits in a desk drawer and few have read it.

As I sit on my perch and place the puzzle pieces together, I think of the man I had named the Baker. A man I met a few months ago who almost died. We have had many conversations over the last few months and one sunk deep into me. I asked if he had moved past the death of his coworkers and he said, "No, I just accepted it." The more I live and the more I feel pain, I can now see that accepting something is one of the first steps in allowing the heart and mind to process that event which has left us with a look of a young boy looking at a concrete pond. Our perception of how life will be, or what our role in life will be, can become very complicated when an event does not match our perceptions. My father learned to accept his cancer. My mother accepted the bad knee and the loss of her husband. My dad was right. The board was as straight as it would ever be so we accepted it for what it was. I have learned to accept my role as a door holder, but I continue to struggle with the outside influences that have come with my role, as this was not my perception of how I thought my life would be.

It's the last night of deer season and I am sitting with my youngest son while my wife is across the farm sitting with my oldest son. The other night, I was called out for work and my oldest son said, "Daddy why don't you wear anything that says who you work for?" My response was, "Your daddy always loves to be camouflaged." I'm proud of who I work for, but I would rather just blend in. Sitting with one of my boys in the woods is more greatly appreciated after having had the privilege of holding the door open for people who have been through a bad event. There are those who want to treat the role of a door holder as a job with protocols and procedures, but how is that possible when life is never the same and we all process differently? We all accept things at different times. Some never accept them and forever their pieces will not be put back together. In life, timing is everything and when we force time it usually ends in failure. Redneck John Travolta waited for the right time, I held the door open and he started to put the pieces back together.

I listen for the shot from my oldest son's rifle, but I hear nothing. I think of his simple words, "I have a lot of the world in me." His way of saying, if I die, Daddy, don't be sad. I think of all the puzzle pieces from the last year and how I have found a place for them in my swamp, but my role as a door holder does not seem to fit, or at least not at the moment. My dreams of helping people and the ability to do it seems to fit perfect, but the outside influences that come with it, do not fit at all.

Its dark now and my youngest son and I get down from our tree stand. We are in a dark pine thicket so I say, "Give me your hand and follow me as we walk through the pines and the underbrush." As I hold his hand I say "Pay attention to what I'm fixin' to say because I will not always be around to tell you." I say, "Every time you get a chance to offer folks a hand and hold the door open for them, do it."

I explain that a very simple act, like offering someone a hand, gives him or her a break from the hard road of life. "If you hold the door open for them, it also gives them a break from the dark days of life." As we walked, I said, "Hold my hand son, I will help you get out of these dark woods because when you grow up, there will be some dark days, and someone will need your hand; maybe you too, would be willing to offer your hand, to help some folks."

- WLV -

Comments on Chapter 5
Importance Of Peer Support

In the comments section of Chapter 4, associated memories are discussed in some detail. Chapter 5 gives us the opportunity to discuss a bit more about how the brain formulates memories and what happens when memories are dissociated instead of associated.

The Door Holder is a story about the importance of peer support. Peer support personnel make a difference in other people's lives - everyday. They educate people about managing life's traumas. Peers have literally saved lives by preventing suicides. Peers provide a listening ear and an understanding mind. Peers bring hope and, in many ways, they help emergency personnel, members of the armed forces and innumerable organizations, companies, institutions, agencies, universities, schools, governmental entities, and individuals to hang on through some very tough times. Sometimes the only things peers can do to help someone is to show up and be there in the midst of the pain, and isolation, and loneliness. Above all, peers bring a heart to cold and dark places and they hold a door open so someone struggling with trauma can have some light and a little relief while they work their way to recovery.

The Door Holder is also a story that provides some insight into what happens when people encounter an event that cannot easily be processed and they get stuck in dissociated memories.

Your Brain

Imagine the following job description: "This is a high per-formance executive management job requiring the coordination and management of complex bio-chemical, emotional, cognitive and physical tasks twenty-four hours a day, year round, no vacations, no holidays, no breaks, and no pay!" None of us would want a job like that, but that is exactly what your brain is doing from its earliest stages of development before birth until you die.

The human brain is a marvelous organ. Constantly on alert to threats in and around us, the brain assesses, analyzes, and processes complex thoughts and then guides, influences, and initiates action. It is as highly sensitive as human tissue goes. In fact, brain tissue is the most sensitive tissue in the human body. Alcohol and many substances of abuse cause significant damage to brain tissue (and quickly too). Toxins, disease, and head trauma can also damage brain tissue. You can disrupt and slow down and befuddle the brain and reduce its effectiveness, but it will continue to function until death.

The brain is bafflingly intricate and deeply complex. It generates our emotions and the most sophisticated thought processes of any animal on earth. It orchestrates biochemical reactions and the movements of the body. It is the storage area for our memories that can be drawn forward, blended with other memories and used to solve elaborate problems. We have only begun to develop our understanding of how the brain works and what happens when the brain is overloaded by extreme stress or becomes dysfunctional for any reason.

Brain's Executive Functions:

The brain's functions are too numerous to list here, but we will discuss three very important executive functions of the brain.

These are three things the brain does exceptionally well:

1. The brain always tries to **complete** every experience.

2. The brain tries to **simplify** everything it en-counters.

3. The brain tries to **categorize** every experience.

Complete

Let's look at the brain's efforts to complete its experiences. The human brain does not like incomplete experiences so it keeps working on them. It can work on many pieces of unfinished business at the same time. It aims at completion so that experiences can be used for action now or properly stored for retrieval later when such information may be needed.

Most of us have lost sleep as our brains kept working through the night to figure something out (complete the experience). When we are looking at ancient ruins, our brains try to develop a picture of how those ruins looked as complete structures in the glory days of old. When reading a mystery book or watching a mystery on TV our brains work hard to solve the mystery before us. Our brains sometimes suggest 'who done it' long before 'who done it' is announced. If we don't get it right, the brain will try to reanalyze the clues and figure out what it missed. When right, our brains do a happy dance (well, sort of). In reality, when our brains complete an experience, the brain sends signals to the body that relax the entire system (job done; take a break). But the brain itself does not take a break. It is the master executive. It is always on. It is always working on something. It takes up the next issue and then the next. It processes each event or issue that comes up. Again, it can work on many things at the same time. If an emergency arises, the brain can snap into action instantaneously and shift focus to managing the emergency. Then it returns to more routine functions when the emergency is over.

Simplify

As complex and powerful as the brain happens to be, it works toward simplicity. It tries for the easy solutions first and if it appears that the simple solutions will not work, the brain then ratchets up its analysis with ever increasingly complex solutions. The brain continues to find the simplest solution as it processes a problem. On the other hand, the brain recognizes that over-simplification can be problematic. Analytically, the brain avoids overly simplistic solutions, but, emotionally speaking, there may be a problem. Sometimes one's emotions engage before the brain has the opportunity to think through the entire issue. Emotions can be pesky and they can be very impulsive. When someone dies, for example, the survivors' brains are highly activated by the shock associated with the death. A loved one may falsely conclude that the death is their fault. Some might say something like, "I was not home and that is why the person died. Had I been here this would not have happened." That narrow, simplistic thinking can cause us a great deal of distress and irrational guilt. Emotional acceptance of an incomplete analysis can interfere with the brain's continued analysis of the situation and it may not be able to simplify the experience or complete it properly at that time.

Categorize

The brain focuses on placing everything into easily retrievable categories. It is a very efficient filing system for everything we encounter. Colors, shapes, events, tragedies, losses, people, families, violence, and just about anything else can be placed into categories by our brains. Smoke at a fire, for example, can be white, black, or colored depending what is burning. Each color of smoke can be its own category. Almost everything can be categorized. The exceptions are experiences that are so far outside the realm of ordinary human experience that the brain cannot find a proper category. The memories from events that do not fit in a specific category are called dissociated memories. The most common cause of dissociated memories is exposure to a severe traumatic event.

The Hamster Wheel

If we can't categorize an experience, then we are left to replay it through our minds in a constant and very long search to place the traumatic experience where it can be put to rest in our minds. Sometimes we cannot achieve that goal and we continue to be distressed by not being able to categorize an experience - perhaps for a lifetime. It is like a hamster running, running, and running on his wheel. The hamster gets little out of the experience except a slim trim figure and exhaustion. But the hamster really gets nowhere. Sometimes we climb onto our own hamster wheels in our heads. We keep trying to find a category for this awful experience we have undergone. We fail despite enormous and long-term efforts. We cannot find peace with whatever happened.

There is a saying in the field of crisis intervention. "A crisis remains a crisis until some resolution is found." It does not matter if the event is five minutes old or fifty years old. If we can't find something that helps us put the experience in perspective, then we cannot resolve it. Without resolution, we have mental pain and no peace. That could last a lifetime.

The brain may not always be successful in its attempts to complete, simplify, and categorize, but it will always keep trying. Part of the problem of disassociated memories is that many times the memories do not fit into any of the existing categories. The memories cannot be associated because they simply do not match up. For example, law enforcement personnel at the scene of a child murder have a hard time categorizing such cruelty toward a child especially if the prime suspect is one of the child's parents. The category is inadequate because it is very far outside of the lifetime experience of the officers. No category really seems to work and the memory remains dissociated and unconnected with the associated memories.

When the brain cannot complete, simplify, or categorize what we experience, the memories of the experience are dissociated. Here are some characteristics of dissociated memories:

- These memories are walled off and separate from associated memories.

- **Associated** memories are like files in a file cabinet organized and interrelated, but **dissociated** memories are like disorganized files thrown on your desktop.

- It is not possible to ignore the memories on your *desk*. They will intrude into consciousness. They are there.

- Dissociated memories demand attention because they are active memories with all of the intense emotions still attached. Active memories don't let up. They keep demanding our attention even when we would rather not deal with them.

- Dissociated memories are highly, emotionally charged.

- Memory fragments are not integrated and they do not blend together as associated memories do.

- Any **trigger** (see comments for Chapter two) can stimulate certain fragments of memory and even some physical discomfort.

- Unspoken and unchallenged distortions sometimes have a grain of truth, but they also come with plenty of exaggerations and distortions too.

- Part of healing is challenging the distortions.

- Healing thoughts from associated memories cannot, without help, penetrate the wall that keeps dissociated memories separate from associated memories.

- A person's identity may split so that a part of them is stuck in a memory and a part is in the present.

- A person may *float away* when distressed or be sucked into a painful aspect of memory and *relive* it or have vivid memories or *flashbacks*.

- The person loses focus on the present.

- During the traumatic event, the prefrontal cortex (thinking, language processes) and the Hippocampus (memory and learning processes) get shut down due to an overload of stress chemicals.

- The Amygdala (it generates the high intensity emotions such as rage, and intense fear, terror) has to take over and it stores memories in a fragmented, isolated manner with intense emotional overtones, particularly anger. The Amygdala is not the best file keeper. It attaches too much harsh emotional attributes to the memories. They remain too active and sometimes become dissociated.

Dissociated Memories vs. Associated Memories

I explained associated and dissociated memories to my 17 year-old daughter, Kyla and asked her to devise a way to depict those concepts. In twenty minutes she came up with the following graphic. The net represents the wall between the organized associated memories and the chaotic dissociated memories. The trigger could be anything distressing that stirs up the dissociated memories (team D). The volleyball signifies an intrusive memory that attempts to penetrate the associated memories. Because associated memories are organized and balanced, they remain in the game and are not overwhelmed as the dissociated memories are by an intrusive memory.

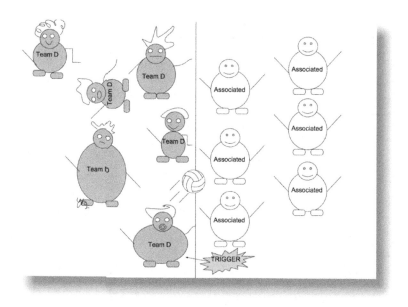

In the "Door Holder" Josey describes the character he nicknames 'Redneck John Travolta.' The guy had a terrible tragedy ten years earlier and he had many dissociated memories of that horrible event. He had never really spoken of it. He hid behind his well-developed sense of firehouse humor. When Josey, in the classroom where Redneck John Travolta sat, told the story of a fire in which the only survivor was a rabbit, he got Redneck's attention. Then he presented Redneck with a plastic rabbit and explained that sometimes we are the rabbit and there is no good explanation as to why we survived and others did not.

The next day, Redneck came forward and told his entire terrible story with a good deal of detail. He took the first steps toward reducing the turmoil left in his life by the story he had refused to tell for so long. He was getting off his hamster wheel and trying to focus on things in his world. He was trying to find a way to get his dissociated memories turned into associated memories. That brought him a bit closer to finding a resolution of his crisis and ultimately to peace. He was buying his freedom from dissociated memories.

Before, I didn't know what my dad went through but now I do. It was bothering me all day. I got very dizzy, when I looked at things I saw the dead body's head and when I looked at people I saw the dead body walking. And I can home and I told my dad about the dead body. He took me back to his room, he showed me stuff I knew, and he showed me stuff I didn't know. Then he took me to his office and taught me about the file cabinet. Your brain is like a file cabinet. And the files are sections in your brain. He said that if you don't know what it is, your brain doesn't know what file to put it in. That's what keeps you thinking about the bad thing. This talk helped me and I don't think about the dead body any more because my dad helped me with it.

Wyatt Visnovske

Young Wyatt Visnovske's distress at seeing a picture of a dead body in a book initiated a period of "hamster wheeling" for him. He kept rethinking the image again and again and he could not find a place to put the image in his mind. He had no peace regarding that image until he talked to Josey and described what he had seen. Instead of making the mistake that only a very few parents might make of dismissing Wyatt's concerns by stating that it was only a picture and not something to be concerned about, Josey cleverly discussed familiar things that Wyatt would remember because they were familiar to him. Josey asked him if he could find certain objects if Josey sent him to look for them. Wyatt said he could because he was familiar with the draw they were stored in. He was at ease because he had learned about those familiar items and had time to become comfortable with them. They were in a certain draw (category).

Josey also showed Wyatt some things he would not be so familiar with. Wyatt was unsure about what those objects were and he needed a little explanation about the unfamiliar items. Josey then asked Wyatt if he could retrieve those objects if he was asked to bring one of them to Josey. Wyatt felt that would be harder because he had not yet learned what the objects were and where exactly they were stored. Josey then moved on and showed Wyatt a file cabinet in his office and explained how things are stored in their own separate files. A file in a file cabinet is similar to a category in the brain. The brain tries to put everything it comes upon into categories from which they can be easily retried. Josey explained that Wyatt was uncomfortable about the image of the dead person because his brain had not yet developed a category or a file where it could be placed. Josey concluded his lesson by letting Wyatt know that it is perfectly normal for a person to be distressed when they first encountered something unfamiliar. Once the brain developed a category for the experience, it would become easier for Wyatt to know what he saw and what it meant. Things became far less disturbing once the brain had a place to put a memory.

- JTM -

Sister Mary, the Baker, the Barber, and the Bricklayer

Chapter 6

The Stairway

Dad and I climbed the long hill in search of the view that he promised me would be awesome. Dad seldom used the word awesome so I knew it was worth my struggle to keep up with his longer legs. Dad pointed over to my right and said, "There used to be an old quarry over there, years ago." Dad worked in a quarry not far from here and even though he did not like blasting into the earth he still talked about quarries a lot. I saw what I thought was an easier way to follow dad and I strayed a little to the right of the trees that he just walked through. I slipped on a loose rock and went head over heels down the hill. I could hear dad yelling something but I was just trying to grab something to stop me from rolling. When I finally came to a stop there were no trees around me and I was on a very steep hill with just rocks. I looked up and could see the trees where we were walking and could still hear dad yelling for me. I looked below me and I was only a few feet from the edge of the quarry. The rocks under me were broken and sharp and I kept slipping towards the edge of the quarry. I was too scared to yell in fear it would make me slip off the edge.

At the top of the hill I finally saw dad and he yelled, "Are you ok?" I nodded my head up and down and he said, "If I crawl down to you I'm afraid it will cause rocks to fall on you, you need to crawl up real slow." Dad never had much to say and his face always kind of looked the same but the look in his eyes was one I had never seen before. I hung there on that hillside like a squirrel hanging on the side of a tree covered in ice. I guess dad thought I did not hear him and he yelled again, "If I crawl down to you I'm afraid it will cause rocks to fall on you, you need to crawl up real slow." This time his voice sounded much different and I had never heard dad sound like that. He was not mad, angry, or sad. It was then I figured out my dad was scared. Every time I would move my boots or hands the rocks under them would move.

Dad tried to move closer to me and a handful of small rocks came rolling down to me. I hung there and realized I needed to do something so I moved my right foot and attempted to climb towards dad but I started to slide down towards the edge. Dad yelled for me to stop moving but I did not listen. I felt like our truck in the cold winter when dad would try and climb the long hill to our house in the snow. I finally got a good grip with my left foot and I crawled up that hill like it was a race. I could hear dad yelling but the rocks falling behind me made it hard to hear him. I had my head down and was focused on getting up the hill when I felt something grab my shirt. I looked up and it was dad. Dad held me in his arms and he was never big about hugging but he was that day. The look in his eyes was still there but it seemed to fade behind his glasses. Dad said, "Let's go home," and I said, "What about the view?" Dad said, "You still want to see the view?" and I said, "Yes sir." We finally made it to the top of the hill and sat on a big rock. Dad said, "See that flat land over there, that's another state, not as nice as our state and they love to come over here because we got hills."

As I crawled up on the overlook I could see the large river below. Across the river were more large hills like the ones behind me. I sat there and could not see another human being. I thought back to that day in the rock quarry and how dad and I never spoke of that day or what had happened. That day was the first time in my life that death showed its face to me and somehow I managed to outsmart it or maybe it was just not my time. It was many years before I truly understood what the look meant on my dad's face that day. The look was fear and helplessness. I have learned to accept the feeling of fear and in many cases fear has kept me alive but the feeling of helplessness is a painful feeling that seldom resolves itself without some type of overt action.

The river below me was at least a quarter mile away. The river brought back the memories of the small river where we spent our summer vacations, except this river was about four times larger.

We had a small cabin we rented for 200 hundred dollars a year. We had cold running water, an outhouse, and no air conditioning. The cabin was one large room with a porch and a deck out back that my dad built. My dad built a set of steps to the river where there was a floating dock. Dad was a pretty good carpenter. I looked hard across the river and the land just never seemed to stop. Today was five years since dad took his last breath. I never say dad died because my mom said, "He took his last breath and let go, after I told him to." I brought mom here on the one-year anniversary of the dad's death. She had never been here and I told her, "This place is magical and can cure what hurts."

I heard someone yell but the voice was lost in this open land. I turned around to the hills behind me and my wife was standing there. She saw me and yelled, "I saw your water bottle on the edge of the cliff and I thought you slipped off the edge." I yelled back, "No I just saw a place to crawl out on and get a better look." I worked my way back up to her and the look in her eyes was fear, but not helplessness. I asked, "Where are the boys?" She said, "Back there playing by the Jeep." My family and I have been coming to this magical place for years. Though it's hard to compete with that one-room fishing cabin where I spent my summers, this place balances me. The beauty or curse of being married to my best friend is no matter how hard we try and hide, conceal, or mask what hurts us – we each know. At that moment I was as open as the land that surrounded us but my best friend never said a word.

The phone rang and one of my coworkers told me he had a fatal fire and wanted to know was I available to help him, I said, "sure." As I prepared my cooler and changed clothes, I thought about how many times I have done this before, but the words "fatal fire" make it something I do not want to turn into a routine.

As I drove the hour to the fire I thought about the research I did years ago on the physiological effects of working fatal fires. I learned a lot about the way my brain and other investigators brains process events that are not routine. There are days I feel I have a handle on how we process these non-routine events and then there are days I feel like I'm on the edge of that rock quarry.

Sister Mary, the Baker, the Barber, and the Bricklayer

As I pull up to the fire, I can smell the bunt house before I get out of my truck. My routine once I arrive at the fire scene is to get my camera ready, change my boots, and put my respirator around my neck. My coworker greets me. He is one that I like so his face immediately calms my fears of what lies inside. He tells me a few things and simply says, "She is in the kitchen." I circle the house taking my pictures and trying to figure out where this beast we call fire decided to make its mark. I've done this so many times it's a routine but once again the words "fatal fire" ring in my head and tell me there is nothing routine about this fire.

As I approach the front door I pull my respirator over my nose and mouth and my breathing changes as I adapt to the breathing through a filter. I tell my boys that we all make tracks in life and we leave our mark. I can see the fire department had to break the door to get in and I can see where this beast called fire waited in the dark, hot house for them to break the door. The beast patiently waited for the fresh, cool air from outside. I took a picture of the smoke stains above the door. As the beast grabbed the cool air, it became stronger.

The house was dark because the smoke dried and covered all the windows. I reached into my right cargo pocket, pulled out and put on my headlamp like I have done hundreds of times. Unlike the fire fighters who entered this house hours ago, I can see and it's not as hot. The fire beast is dead. With my light I see that the fire damage is greater towards the ceiling. In the living room, every thing is covered in baked on smoke. The first drop of sweat rolls down my face and gets tangled up in my respirator. I can hear my respirator filtering the hot air I'm trying to breathe. As I look around the room I take pictures of the things that tell me what the beast was doing while it was in this room. My light lands on an object that instantly causes me to stop. I move closer to make sure it's what I think it is. The object is a folded American flag in a shadow box. The shadow box is coated with baked on smoke but appears to have survived the wrath of the beast.

The research I did told me my worlds just collided. I came up with a term called collision of worlds. It's when your personal life collides with your work life. I stood there with more sweat beads rolling down my face and recalled the day at the funeral home when the man handed my mom the folded up American flag and a fancy jar of what was left of my dad. Days later I bought mom a shadow box to keep the flag in and I'm not sure if I ever wrapped my head around dad being in some fancy jar when an old Ball Mason jar would have suited him fine. I teach new investigators the signs and symptoms when a fatal fire is hitting home and, at that moment, I felt like the battered front door to this house.

I continued from room to room in the house and it was dark like a tomb or cave but not cool. I saw a wooden chest in one room that was covered in dried smoke but not burned by the beast. The chest reminded me of the one my mother has and once again my worlds collided. I felt like I was going deeper into the cave and not leaving a rope behind to find my way out. I continued through the house taking pictures as my mind tried to process the fear of what lies ahead. I could see the marks where fire fighters drag their glove covered hands down the walls because the walls guide them through the cave as they search for the beast and the victims the beast has left behind. As I took a picture of the kitchen, the camera flash lit up the room up and there she was. My coworker told me she was in the kitchen but no words or neon signs can prepare us for the victims of the fire beast. My breathing changed which is normal and I've learned that is a good thing. On the kitchen counter was a large stainless bowel. The same kind of bowl my mom used in our one room cabin to bread the fish we caught out of the river.

A few months ago my mom and my boys returned to the place where the cabin stood many years ago. I had not been back there in 25 years. A bad storm caused the river to rise and it destroyed our cabin and many others. My mom wanted to go back there and see if the steps dad built down to the river were still there. The cabin sat in a large valley between two hills. The valley was a good quarter mile wide and around a hundred acres. As we drove down the gravel road I recalled the many trips on this road riding in the extended cab of our Ford pickup truck. The dust blew in the back seat and I watched my dad hold the wheel like he was the captain of a great ship. We pulled up to the gate to the cabin and I told mom it was locked. She said, "We will walk over there." I said, "Mom it's a long walk and its really hot out." I offered to walk over and search for Dad's steps and she said, "Ok." I asked my boys if they wanted to go with me and they said, "No we will stay with Crazy Grandma." Years ago my boys named her Crazy Grandma and the name fit her well. Though she is an adult, she is a child at heart and my boys have been able to relish in what I got from her as a son.

I crossed the gate and walked the road where I rode my bike on as a kid. The road was still sandy and had not changed in 25 years. In the distance I could see the tree line that marked where the river was and where the cabins once stood. The road was not used like it was when I was a kid and once I got to the river, the road stopped. I tangled my way through the weeds and briars as sweat poured down my face. I kept an eye out for the rattlesnakes that were my fear when I was a kid and I played here. I stretched my neck out and there she was, the river. The place where we caught fish to eat, took our baths, ran limb lines at night, and moms fried fish could be smelled for miles up and down that river. I wanted to jump in the river and ask her if she missed me. I wanted her to know that I did not forget her I just got busy. I worked my way down the bank looking for dad's steps but the trees were so much bigger than I remember. I remember our cabin was about the only one that had a cedar tree growing next to it. I found a large cedar and made my way back to the riverbank. I slid down the bank through brush and, like a gift under a Christmas tree; there were dad's steps. Dad's steps had seen better days but they had survived many a flood beast. I sat there tangled in the brush and could see dad swinging his East Wing hammer as he drove nail after nail to build steps so we could get to her, the river. She was good to us and provided us with memories you cannot buy. I found a piece of a board that was loose and pulled it from the steps. I thought my mom would like that. I got my cell phone out to call my mom and tell her of my success but it displayed no service. I started to walk back and I could see through the heat mirage my boys standing at the gate.

They waved and I waved back. As I crossed the gate they told me that Crazy Grandma has been doing a lot of crying. I kneeled down to my boys because kids and dogs like to be talked to at their level. I said, "Boys we made lots of memories down here and even though this was not a lot of fun for you, in life you sometimes do things for other people and sometimes you do things for yourself. I did not need to come back here but Crazy Grandma wanted to see if Grandpa's steps were still here. A big flood came and destroyed 15 cabins, out buildings, steps, and docks but Grandpa's steps survived, it may mean nothing to you but means everything to her." I handed my mom the piece of wood and for a brief moment we were back in the funeral home with flag and fancy jar in hand. My boys and mom stood next to the gate with wood in hand as I took a picture. As we drove away I said good-bye to the river and promised her I will come back sooner next time.

I continued to follow the path of the beast and soon I found the room where it made its mark. I looked around the room and spoke with my coworker and we had no answers. The beast was hungry in this room and almost consumed everything in it. We knew this is where the beast made its mark. The why would be forever with us and we have learned to live with that unknown, but we will never accept it. I looked out the front door and saw the family standing there behind the tape. I know the look, the look of *why* and I could not answer that. Every mirror in the house was covered in dried on smoke but I did not need to see myself to know my look was the same one my dad had long ago at the rock quarry, helplessness. I teach the newer investigators to stay in their lane—that means work the scene and let someone else work with the family. It's a lot easier to process these non-routine events if you stay in your lane but sometimes in order to calm the feeling of helplessness you have to do something for yourself or others.

I walked to my truck and got a bottle of cleaner and towels. I walked back into the living room and set them on the dining room table. I started to clean the shadow box that held the flag and realized it would be easier outside where I could see and not wear a respirator but a part of me wanted to make this hard. My coworker yelled and said, "What are you doing?" I said, "Something that needs to be done." He replied, "That's why I called you." I cleaned the shadow box and walked outside to the family and said, "I'm sorry and I cleaned it the best I could." The daughter said, "That was my dad's flag, thank you." I asked, "Is there anything you would like me to get?" She said, "A hope chest full of things mom wanted us to have." I went back into the house and with the help of my coworker we carried it out. We sat it on the ground and it was completely black. I removed my respirator and opened it up and the smell of cedar found its way into my nose. Somehow the contents of the hope chest survived the beast.

The drive home was like most drives coming home from a fire, I was tired, hot, and my body smelled of smoke but not the kind we get from a camp fire. This smoke smell is from the beast when it takes those we love. I changed clothes when I got home and told my boys I was headed to the farm to get a run in before dark. My oldest said, "Can I come along?" I said, "Sure" but I really wanted to be alone. The farm is a half-mile behind the house. I did not say two words to my son as we drove there. We parked at the shed and he said, "I will do some mowing while you run." I ran my route through the woods and before long it was dark. I had my headlamp on my head but left it turned off. I wanted to be in the dark. I wanted my feet to connect me to the earth and not my light. I thought hard about the family. I thought hard about the *why*. I knew what I did with the flag and hope chest was for me and not the family. I needed to not feel so damn helpless. I needed to know I provided them some form of relief even though I did not have the *why*. On the ride home I told my son that today was a hard day. He said, "Do you like your job?' I said, "I love my job just that some days are hard and in order to get through days like today, I need to run through the woods, write, and feel I made a difference."

It's been weeks since that fire and my mind has done its best to process that non-routine event. I think often of that hope chest and flag and how most people who have a series of letters behind their name would have told me to stay in my lane. I guess they are right but for those of us that smell the smoke, feel the heat, and are overwhelmed by that feeling of helplessness or is helplessness an emotion, we do what we have to do so we can keep doing this. Sometimes we have to do what is honorable and not sensible even when we know it will make it hurt more. When it becomes routine and no longer hurts, when we no longer search for open land, old rivers, runs in the dark, or the simple words that flow faster than I can chicken-peck out on this computer, it's will be time to hang up my respirator. We will not always have the answers and I know now why my dad never spoke of that day in the rock quarry. The feeling or emotion called helplessness must be felt, it can never be explained. There will be days the cave or tomb is darker, but as the contents of the hope chest survived the beast called fire, as my dad's steps survived the beast called a flood, and as a small boy survived the beast called the quarry, we continue on.

My boys just told me as we climbed into the deer stand, "I don't think Crazy Grandma can climb ladders like she used to, do you think we could build steps for her?" I said, "Sure I knew a guy once who was really good with an East Wing hammer and he taught me a thing or two about building steps."

- WLV-

Comments on Chapter 6

Collision of Worlds

In the comments section for Chapter 3, the issue of Collision of Worlds was discussed in some detail. It may be helpful, at this point, to quickly review the collision of worlds concept. It occurs when our personal and work worlds bang into each other or when our moral code comes up against something we feel uncomfortable about. The story of the Stairway is an excellent example of the collision of worlds. The folded flag in the shadow box, in the home he is investigating, is a powerful collision of worlds for Josey as it reminds him of his dad and his mom. The honor guard gave an American flag to his mother at his father's burial. The bowl on the kitchen counter in the victim's home reminds him of the bowl his mother used to bread the fish that he caught in the river near his boyhood vacation home. The collision of worlds pops up frequently in the story of the Stairway.

Feeling Helpless

Josey also introduces the emotion of helplessness in the story. He tells us that his father looked fearful and helpless when Josey was sliding down the hillside toward a deep quarry. A few years later his wife looked fearful although not helpless under a different set of circumstances. He himself felt helpless when he observed the family outside of the burned out house he was investigating. When he felt helpless, something inside him moved him to action. He crossed a line that most of us are warned not to cross. Sometimes, something deeply human makes us do what we have mostly likely been warned not to do.

Crossing the Line

Whether it's a nursing school, an EMT class, a law enforcement academy, a professional psychology program, a military boot camp, or a fire service training program, someone with many years of experience tells us something like "stay in your lane" or "don't get personally involved with the people you are trying to help." We all get warned that crossing the line can have *harmful effects* on us and, sometimes, to really scare us from doing anything above and beyond the call, *possibly even on those we are trying to help*. We hear the warnings and we try really hard to follow them. After all, those wise, ancient ones know better than us and they have lived the life that gives them the right to tell us not to do something.

Then, like the police office in New York City who bought a pair of boots for a cold, homeless man, or the EMT in Maryland who bought a McDonald's meal for a man down on his luck, or the soldier running into the line of fire to save a wounded buddy, we find ourselves doing something that comes from the deeply human side of us that we have been previously warned to ignore. We take the risk of doing things that make us vulnerable to our own feelings. Our actions can, at times, jeopardize our safety and our lives. Diving into a frozen river to save a drowning woman, or standing up against an armed bully are not necessarily our wisest choices. But, as an injured firefighter once said, "Sometimes you have to do what is right, not necessarily what is smart."

Crossing the line makes us vulnerable to some good things and to some not so good things. On the positive side, those who gave us those early warnings know, first hand, how our feelings of helplessness can be dampened by doing what we believe is the *right thing to do*. They know full well that becoming vulnerable can also simultaneously make us more human. We can feel satisfied that we made a real difference for others at some crucial moment in time. We know full well when we did the honorable thing—the right thing. Without doubt there are positive aspects of crossing the poorly defined line they warned us about.

Here are some of the negative aspects of doing something unusual for others. We get to feel the pain of those in need. We may have to carry, in our minds, the memory of another frightened, grieving person who desperately needed someone to give just a little bit more.

I think the warnings from our instructors come most vigorously when they too have, at some point in their careers, crossed that nebulous line. They know that they felt compelled to do something in the face of chaos, and they acted.

Their warnings to us arise out of concern for our welfare. The people who taught us also knew how distressing it could be to bear the pain of others. Our instructors knew, when we were sitting in their classrooms, that, in some cases, we might bear the wounds from those human encounters, sometimes for the remainder of our lives.

Back to Helplessness

Helplessness is the feeling of "I don't know what to do" or "There is nothing I can do" when we believe deep down that we should be able to do something. Helplessness is one of the **Dirty Dozen**. *I use that term to imply a harmful effect of certain emotions or psychological states.*

All human beings experience a wide range of emotions and psychological states. We do it all the time. Having and using our emotions is natural and normal. The emotions themselves are not bad or dirty. When we use our emotions they keep us healthy both mentally and physically. It is the effects of *not* having, or ignoring, or simply not using our emotions that is *dirty* part. When we do not use them, there are consequences, some of which can make our lives miserable.

Emotions are there even when we do not recognize them and avoid using them as they were designed by God and nature to be used. Big problems arise when we let the emotions take over control of the thinking processes in our brains. If we get overwhelmed by or stuck in our emotions, things are likely to go wrong. It's like letting your seven-year-old drive your brand new pick-up truck through heavy traffic during an ice storm. The outcome probably won't be pretty.

Don't let your emotions get you bogged down. Don't wallow in the emotions. That leads to feeling sorry for you. Don't deny emotions that are pretty evident to everyone else. The negative effects on your life and the people you care about are the dirty parts. Unexpressed, denied, or hidden emotions get stuffed down inside us and then our thinking and interactions with other people get off track. We can hurt others and ourselves when we let our emotions disrupt our thinking. The dirty consequences of unexpressed emotions bind our energy, lock us in an emotional cage, and cause us to be irrational in our behaviors and insensitive to the needs of people who love us.

"Dirty Dozen"

Here is a list of the emotional and psychological states that are most likely to be denied, buried, or ignored. They are also very likely to make many aspects of our lives get dirty if they get buried inside of us. That is, they can divert us from our goals, bind up our energy, block our decision-making, and cause us to be focused on ourselves, or to strike out verbally or physically and hurt people around us.

1. **Helpless or powerless.** Not knowing what to do or feeling as though one could not do anything.
2. **Guilt.** Commonly know as the *Should-a, Could-a* and *Would-as*. I should have done this; I could have done that; I would have done this instead. It is one of the most destructive, disruptive and dangerous of the Dirty Dozen. In some cases, suicide has been the ultimate and unnecessary end point for people suffering excessive guilt.

3. **Hapless.** The person feels that bad things just keep happening to them one after another as if they are being singled out for punishment. It makes them feel isolated and it causes feelings of self-pity.

4. **Hopeless and a loss of future orientation / despair.** The feeling is that there is no hope for me. I am stuck in this situation and there is no way out. The future is blank. The

result may be inactivity, no energy, and a wait for the end of life. Hopelessness is one of the most common driving forces in suicide.

5. **Worthless / loss of self–esteem.** The person feels that they have no value and that no one would care for them since they are so worthless. Some describe feelings of self-loathing or self-hatred. It is closely associated with suicidal thoughts and actions.

6. **Fear.** It escalates up from specific fears to generalized fear. It kind of sucks the life out of us and we lock down into frozen over-control. If you are interested in doing nothing, fear can help you to do that.

7. **Anger, Revenge, Blind Rage.** Anger interferes with rational thought. Common sense becomes less common. Anger diverts energy to un-important slide-line issues. Unresolved anger sets the stage for revenge. All we want to do then is pay somebody back for what they did to us. 'Round and round she goes. Where it stops, nobody knows.' Blind rage is totally irrational and can lead you right to a prison cell.

8. **Anxiety and agitation.** This is a condition of worry and over-concern for us and for our family and friends. We look for threats everywhere. It is exhausting and not very effective!

9. **Denial.** A disaster writer by the name of Dustin wrote in the 1970s, "Denial in the face of obvious fact indicates terror." It blocks us from even recognizing a problem. We fear to admit a problem because admitting that a problem exists means we should do something about it. Denial generates fear that we might not be able to handle the problem.

10. **Unrelenting Grief.** Loss just plain hurts, physically and psychologically. Sometimes we prefer to push it down inside and we wall people out because we fear that they could not possibly understand what we feel and that they

cannot help us deal with our loss. It makes us angry because we simply do not like what life has dolled out to us. We resent anyone who is happy in his or her relationships because it reminds us that we were once happy ourselves. Now we are not and sad is a dark place to be.

11. **Humiliation.** Feeling humiliated or belittled can make us angry and resentful or it can make us react with hurt, depression, and a loss of self-esteem.

12. **Ambiguity.** Uncertainty presents a challenge. We cannot decide one way or the other, but a decision must be reached. Some people even agonize over decisions while losing sleep and growing more irritable. They feel unstable and confused. Thinking becomes a burden and they may give up altogether.

Remember, we all go through these emotional / psychological states. Sometimes they can even help us. For example, ambiguity can allow us a little time to consider the options before finally making a decision. Having and using the emotions is not the bad thing. Not allowing our selves to experience the emotions or getting caught up too deeply in them is the real problem.

Any of these dirty dozen psychological states can combine with one or more of the others and cause deeper, more complex, and more destructive consequences.

The formula for success in managing these emotions and their harmful consequences is to recognize and acknowledge one's emotions and to express them in a controlled and appropriate manner. Telling our story about what happened to us and discussing who or what we lost or how agonized or terrified we were releases the pain and helps us to be free to live again.

- JTM -

Sister Mary, the Baker, the Barber, and the Bricklayer

Chapter 7

The Baker, the Barber, and the Bricklayer.

I sat there with the old towel wrapped around my shoulders and the sound of the hair clippers buzzing in my ears. My mom told me to hold still or she would cut my ear off. Our barbershop was always in the kitchen and mom was our barber. I was not sure if she was trained to cut hair but she did ours and also cooked our meals.

The next morning at 5 a.m., I could hear my dad tapping the broom handle on the floor under my bedroom. He yelled, "You better get moving we don't need to be late." Our barbershop was now a kitchen again and mom had made breakfast and had packed our lunch boxes. My dad was dressed in his Wrangler jeans and long sleeve denim shirt. I was wearing my old military surplus camouflage pants and a t-shirt I cut the sleeves off of. We drove the 25 miles in his truck with no air conditioning and our lunch boxes sat between us. Dad's lunch box had some duct tape on it and mine was much newer. As we rolled down the river hills to the cement plant that had been my dad's job for over 20 years dad said, "Be careful today."

I had a full time job before this but quit to work this summer with my dad and make more money. I was going to college full time so the cement plant hired me as summer college labor. My job at the cement plant was doing manual labor. That meant using a shovel and running a jackhammer. My dad worked in the quarry where he drilled holes in the earth and blasted rock to be made into cement. I shoveled the loose rock into the wheelbarrow and rolled it to the edge of the silo. My hardhat, safety glasses, and earplugs were things I could not seem to get used to. When I reached the edge of the roof the safety rope attached to my safety harness pulled tight. I lifted the two handles on the wheelbarrow and waited before I dumped it to the ground below. The ground was roped off with yellow safety tape and the rain the night before left a large puddle. I saw the clean white shirt and tan pants of the safety officer. I knew him well; his wife had taught me in the sixth grade. As the safety officer approached the safety tape I dumped my wheelbarrow and before he could move the dirty water covered his white shirt. By the time he recovered from his dirty bath I was away from the roof edge and I was just another laborer working at the cement plant that day. On the ride home that evening I told my dad of the dirty bath I gave the safety officer and dad never laughed but he smiled. At the end of the summer the cement plant offered me a full time job but dad told me to stay in school and get a job I love.

Years later, I was getting ready for bed and my wife asked me if I was going to deer hunt in the morning and I said, "Yes." A few minutes later I received a text message that requested volunteers to work a scene where several men died and others were injured. I responded to the text and said, "Yes." As I stood at the baggage claim and waited for my all my bags, I wondered if this one would be any different than the ones before this. Anyone who decides to become a first responder, police officer, or fire fighter learns quickly that the term LODD stands for Line-of-Duty-Death. We all know it's a dangerous job but somehow we forget how human we are.

As I unpack my bags in the hotel room I remove my hardhat and steel-toed boots. I reach into my pocket and clip on the back of my hardhat two things given to me by my sons for good luck. My hardhat and boots are much fancier than the ones I wore in the cement plant, but that was over 30 years ago. Even though I went to college like dad asked me to, I somehow came full circle and found that after many years of carrying a gun to protect others, the shovel in my hand seems to fit better. The next morning I found myself in a room with some people I knew and some I had never met before. I always looked at their boots. I looked to see if they were new or were they worn.

It's hard to describe the sadness that's in the air but under the sadness is a degree of energy caused by those who feel better with a shovel in their hands, those who seek to answer the why question. We all know why we choose to come here because it's an honor to dig for the answers, but the real why is, "Why did this have to happen." As we sit with anticipation like being in a waiting room in a hospital and hear about why we were brought here, we can only imagine the place that will become our home for the days to come.

I stood outside the safety yellow tape and my faded uniform, hard hat, and boots tell the police officer in front of me I have a right to be there. I grabbed the yellow safety tape in my hand and it felt the same no matter where I went. Even in the heat of summer the tape was always cold and even though it's plastic it had an edge like a knife. I lifted the yellow safety tape up and my body crawled under it and now the digging began. The days were long and with hardhat, respirator, and safety glasses on we all looked the same. When the heavy equipment was not close by I could hear the two things my sons gave me that were clipped to my hardhat. That small noise made by the two metal items banging together on my helmet was a constant reminder of the world outside this tape. As we dug through the collapsed building I never thought I would have gone to college to pick up bricks. I never thought picking up bricks would be the job of honor it had turned out to be.

I stood up one day to stretch my back from being bent over and in the distance behind the tape stood a man and his wife. The man looked at the pile of debris as if he had lost something there. I looked over to my boss and he motioned for me. As I crossed the street I removed my hardhat and respirator. The fresh air felt good against my face and head. My boss explained to me that I needed to walk the man around the collapsed building. He explained that the man was here when it happened. I had done this before so I knew what to expect. The last time I did it I felt like I was in charge of a time machine that could take these poor damaged souls back to the place where *it* happened. I think I had the same feeling this time too.

When they were here, just a few nights before, it all seemed to be under control. The bricks were still a wall and not yet a pile. A second later the control was gone and the nightmare began. As we walked around the building he reminded me of my sons on their first day of school. They wanted me to know how strong they were, but inside I could tell they would rather just go back home where it was familiar and safe. He had the humor that most first responders have, and I too have that humor, but under all that humor lied a whiff of the raw side of life that only humor can mask.

As we approached the spot where his nightmare began my time machine stopped with a powerful force. His humor was gone in a flash and the fear in his eyes was much more intense than the look in my sons' eyes as I let go of their hands on that first day of school. As we finished our walk around the building, I wanted to sit down with him and talk but my debris pile was calling me. I asked him to wait for me for a moment as I went to my car to get him something. As I crossed the grass parking lot he stood there like a concrete statue watching me and hoping I had the answers to unlock the footlocker that just had more added to it. I had only spoken to him for a few minutes but my gut told me what I was about to tell him was what he needed. I did not try to make him feel better. I just simply said a few words to him but they were from the heart.

I handed him a small plastic rabbit and told him the story of how a whole family died but their pet rabbit survived. I told him he could spend the rest of his life trying to make sense of this event or just be the rabbit and survive. I told him of the weeks, months and years to come. I told him this event "can destroy you or define you. It's your choice, now you are back in control." As I crossed under the tape he once again stood there like a concrete statue watching me. I could tell a part of him wanted to join me as I searched for answers in the debris pile but I could also tell he gave all he could give the other night when the debris pile was made.

The next day I was back in my pile of debris searching for answers when I felt my phone vibrate. I answered the phone and it was the man from the day before. He asked, "Did you mean what you said yesterday?" I said, "Yes, every word." He said, "I woke up last night and was having trouble sleeping and looked at that stupid rabbit and not sure why but I realized I can survive this." He said, "Do you have plans for supper?" and I said, "No."

At the end of day I felt like I had something to look forward to besides the food I had crammed in my mini fridge in the hotel room. I have never been big on going out to eat with my coworkers especially on a LODD. I love my job digging for answers but on a LODD I just feel guilty when I enjoy my job when so many have to suffer.

As I pulled up to his house the American flag on his front porch snapped in the wind as if to remind me freedom is never free. I knocked on the door and explained my boots were very dirty and so was the rest of me. He said take off your boots and I will give you a pair of shorts to wear. As I entered his home, the smell of supper over took me, and the odor of burnt wood and busted bricks left me. It was if he was now in charge of the time machine and he was taking me back to that barbershop kitchen that I had left many years ago. He proceeded to explain to me the food he had prepared and the cheesecake he had made. I knew at that point his name would be "the Baker." We sat around the kitchen and ate and laughed. I told them stories of who I am and the places I had been. We never talked about why I was there. They already knew that answer. Over the week that followed there were many more meals and laughs around that table. As if my life had gone back in time from the cement plant during the day to the barbershop kitchen at night. I knew the time machine was working when I found myself getting a hair cut in the Baker's kitchen as his wife buzzed the trimmers around my ears. I knew at that point her name would be "the Barber."

I wiped my helmet clean of the dust and placed my boots in a plastic bag. I zipped up my bag and drove towards the airport. I stopped at the Baker's house for one last laugh. I told him I would stay in touch and he walked me to the door. Like the first day of school I could tell he did not want me to leave, but he knew I had to go.

I flew half way across the county so I could do a training video on what it's like to work a LODD. The training video had been planned months prior to this event. I really wanted to just go home. I missed my wife and sons. I missed my dog. I missed the woods. I boarded the plane and the man next to me thanked me for serving our county. I wore nothing that said I had but some things you just cannot hide. I leaned my head against the widow in the plane and thought of the Baker. I thought of how he never mentioned the piles of debris that coated his body and how his coworkers had to dig him out. He never spoke of the physical pain he was in and it was not my job to tell him the emotional pain would always be there. I woke when the plane landed and the man next to me said, "Son I've never seen someone sleep through turbulence like that." I said, "Yes sir I'm a little tired and just want to go home."

The next morning I found myself being interviewed on video about what it's like to work a LODD. I could not decide if the burnt smell and dust still inside my nose was there so this interview would seem as real as the place I had just come from. I struggled with my words but simply said it was an honor to work an LODD but I wanted to go home.

Once again when the plane landed I woke up. I found myself waiting for my bags at the baggage claim. The drive home was longer than normal but the roads seem to guide me. The house was dark as I pulled up. It was late. As I opened the door, my dog's wet nose greeted me and he had many kisses to give me. The house smelled familiar and it felt good to be home.

I walked back to my sons' room and covered them up and kissed the oldest on his head. As I kissed the youngest on his head the time machine went fast forward and it finally dawned on me that one of the firefighters who did not walk away will never kiss his children on the head again. I slid down the side of his bed and sat on the floor and cried. I'm not sure how long I sat there but I cried and cried.

A few months later and miles from the Baker, my sons and I were on an annual canoe float trip with my aging mother. We pulled our canoes up on a rock bar and my youngest son yelled for me. He had found a brick in the rocks and asked if we could take it home. I said, "Sure." As he handed me the brick I thought of the Baker and how many bricks it took to bring him down. How a brick prior to meeting the Baker was for building things not destroying them.

I stayed in touch with the Baker and the Barber because I know that those who survive a LODD also need support. They need someone to give them an idea of what they will have to go through. In a sense, survivors of trauma need a 'mental roadmap' to guide them through the tough times. It is easier to work it out if you have some idea what you will have to go through. I worked another LODD many years ago and I stay in fairly constant contact with many from that one. I have learned what most people want is not to be forgotten.

The months that followed the night the Baker found himself face down, started to reveal the physical trauma his body absorbed. He was unable to return to work and had to have several surgeries. A man who provided for his family was now a man being driven around from doctor appointment to doctor appointment. A man who could stand his ground, a man who put his life before others was now sitting on the sofa. On rare occasions, the Baker would speak of what bothered him and he told me he felt guilty for complaining that he could not work because at least he was still here.

Over the next year I would make trips to see the Baker and the Barber. There were times the sofa life was getting the best of him and there was nothing I could do about it but be his friend and make him laugh.

My phone rang one evening and we were eating supper but I said, "I need to take this." I walked outside and it was the Baker. He said, "I turned my papers in today." He said, "The doctors will not release me to go back to work so I did not have much of a choice." The Baker made a joke or two and then said, "I'm not sure where I would be if you did not come along and said what you said." I stood in the dark outside my home miles from him but I could see his face like the first time I saw him. I asked to myself, "Whoever is driving the time machine now, will you please pick up my friend the Baker and make sure he finds his way back home?"

The Baker, the Barber, and all the others who I have met on LODD's will forever be a part of my life. Tragedy brought us together but our love of our country, doing the right thing, responding to those in need, and the pain we endured along the way bonded us like cement. It is truly an honor to be a part of an LODD but one's body and mind absorb the trauma just like the Baker did when hit with the debris. My dad blasted the earth to make cement for roads, buildings and anything that requires a solid bond. I dig through the debris for answers as to why sometimes the debris takes some from us. I gave the lone brick my son found in the river a home when I placed it on our mantel. It reminds me of our constant need to rebuild when tragedy has struck. When I'm not digging for answers then I guess I'm a "Bricklayer" helping our fallen survivors to have a solid place to stand where they will never be forgotten.

- WLV -

Comments on Chapter 7

"The Baker, the Barber and the Bricklayer" is a great story about peer support. It is rich in important peer support concepts, cautions, and guidelines to help peers do it right. The story covers many of Josey's most important peer support principles.

Josey's Peer Support Principles

1. **Show-up. Be there.** You can't make an impact on anybody if you avoid contact with those in need of support or if you rush in and rush out.
2. **Commit. Take the oath of care.** It is not about you. If you don't care, don't be there.
3. **Don't try to make them feel better.** Your job is to help them search for their own answers, not give them your answers.
4. **Let them drive.** They have to guide the intervention, not us. It is when they are ready, not when we are ready.
5. **People in a state of crisis universally hate "Forced-talking."** It has little effect other than to make the person angry and resentful. Ultimately, they will reject you and your "help."
6. **Peer support is not a one-stop.** It is **not** once and done.
7. **Support can be almost anything.** Your presence may help; a few carefully timed simple words may help; a kind gesture may be all that is necessary. Each person and each situation is different.
8. **Just because it worked before, does not mean it will work now.** There are no cookie cutters in peer support. Thinking it through and innovation are key elements in peer support services.
9. **Timing is critical.** Too early and those who need your help are not ready. Too late, they will wonder where you were when you were really needed.

10. **Some events are sticky.** When you finish your peer support, some events will stick to you for a long time, if not forever.

Repetitive Themes

There is an old adage in the field of education and it goes like this, "In repetition, there is learning." In the comments section of Chapter 6 we covered many issues including the collision of worlds, Feeling Helpless, Crossing the Line, and the Dirty Dozen. These topics and many others do not just show up in only one of Josey's stories. They are repetitive themes. They arise from time to time in several of his stories. These themes not only show up in the stories. They appear in classes that Josey teaches and in the conversations he has had with traumatized people. They frequently ask him questions about the themes. Sometimes certain themes play a major role in a story. Sometimes their role is hardly noticeable. In any case, if we pay attention, the themes give us great insights into the power of peer support. The slight repetition of themes from one story to another can help us to learn the important lessons of peer support.

Helplessness

In the story of "The Baker, the Barber, and the Bricklayer," both Josey and the Baker have strong feelings of helplessness, but they have them from totally different perspectives. The Baker feels helpless in light of the death of colleagues. Josey feels helpless because he is uncertain of how he can help this man who lost his friends and came so close to death himself. Josey crossed the line that is symbolically represented by the yellow safety tape. When he crossed that line he came in contact with a deeply pained firefighter who was immersed in helplessness and guilt, which are some of the dirty dozen emotional or psychological states described in the comments section for section six. That firefighter needed reassurance and information. He was suffering affective and cognitive starvation (see affective and cognitive sections below in this comments chapter 7).

Fatigue

As he flew home from the line-of-duty-death investigation, Josey slept through severe turbulence as evidenced by the man sitting next to him, who told him he had never seen anyone sleep through such shaking. Human beings must have sleep to maintain their health and their ability to perform day-to-day activities and to keep their minds clear and functional. Sleep deprivation has an enormous negative impact on people.

Lack of sleep has physical consequences. We can become dizzy, experience headaches, become unsteady in our walking, and our fine motor control becomes erratic. Visual acuity may deteriorate. Heart rate, blood pressure, pulse and breathing can be altered. Gastro-intestinal problems may arise. This is a short list. There are many more physical manifestations of sleep deprivation.

Not getting enough sleep causes cognitive dysfunction. Without sleep, we can't think straight. Our memory becomes impaired. It is harder to problem solve, analyze our circumstances, or make decisions. Sleep deprivation causes us difficulties in name-recognition, mathematical calculations, abstract thinking, and we make many more mistakes than when we are rested.

The emotional consequences of sleep deprivation are impressive. Anger and irritability goes way up and we develop "hair triggers" to minor, inconsequential stimuli. We become more easily frustrated. Anxiety, insecurity, loss of self-esteem, lowered self-image, fear, loss of emotional control and phobic reactions are pretty common in sleep deprivation. So is an increasing level of depression. For peer support personnel, sleep deprivation makes us more vulnerable to strong emotions that are generated by contact with people in distress.

We tend to identify more strongly with those who are emotionally wounded and broken. When Josey returned home after a long deployment at the scene of a fatality fire involving line-of-duty-death and a video production on the same topic, he was physically and mentally exhausted. The simple act of kissing his children on the head reminded him that men, from the scene he had just worked as an investigator, would never kiss their children again. This was a collision of worlds for him between his work as a certified fire investigator and his personal life as a dad and husband. He was quickly overwhelmed with grief and sat on the floor between his children's beds and cried.

Behavioral problems also appear in the absence of sleep. We tend to withdraw from others. We avoid people, places and circumstances that are distressful even when our jobs call for us to be responsive to those things. At the other extreme, we might do things that are inherently dangerous to us because we see someone in distress and feel that internal drive, not to stand by and feel helpless, but to engage in helping behaviors. Sleep deprivation makes us impulsive. With more sleep we might have thought our actions through more thoroughly before acting. Then again, without sleep deprivation we would probably have fewer medal-of-honor awardees.

Collateral Damage

Trauma work causes collateral damage. Emergency and military personnel go into harm's way and they do their jobs and return home. Their spouses and children did not enter harms way, but they recognize that their dads and moms are a little different than they were before they were deployed. The reactions of their moms and dads to the trauma they witnessed have an effect on the children. Collateral damage.

In a similar manner, peer support personnel assist emergency, military personnel and others in the aftermath of trauma. They hear the detailed stories. There is no doubt, they absorb some of what they see and hear and taste and feel and then they transmit the distress to the family and friends they love the most. You cannot work in the trauma field and not be touched by the things you have seen and the people you have met. Collateral damage.

Gallows Humor

Josey refers to the humor that both he and the Baker used even on their first meeting and practically every time they met thereafter.

He acknowledged that humor masks the raw side of life. It is called black humor or "Gallows" humor. Most emergency personnel have some humor that they share with their colleagues. This type of humor is healthy and protective as long as it is used in a defensive manner and not in an aggressive, offensive manner. Emergency services personnel are not the only people to use humor to protect themselves from trauma and tragedy. I have frequently had the privilege to be around military personnel. There are times my sides hurt from laughing at their antics. It was not hard to conclude that at least some of their humor camouflaged the pain of losing a fellow soldier.

Humor as a defense mechanism appears in many professions. Nurses, physicians, technicians, pilots, prison staff, teachers, and a host of others use humor to protect themselves from the stress and turmoil of life. It is not sick or abnormal. It is just people trying to get through a tough shift so that they can go home and leave the turmoil and chaos behind for a little while.

Recommended Crisis Contacts

In peer support, three to five contacts with a distressed person are the normally recommended level of crisis intervention interactions. When you reach six, seven or eight contacts, you should be considering a referral. If you get to nine, ten, eleven or twelve contacts referral is indicated. These are good recommendations and they work to our benefit in most cases. Every once in a while, peers run into a circumstance that may require longer and more involved contact with someone who needs support. In some cases the distressed person adamantly refuses to accept a referral. Leaving them to work it out on their own can have disruptive and harmful consequences. In other cases, there are no resources available near the person in need of help and the peer must do what they can for a period of time until the person stabilizes after the critical incident.

A naval officer friend once told me, "Under extraordinary circumstances, ordinary rules of engagement no longer apply." There are times when a peer has to cross that line and engage with a suffering person for a bit longer time than is normally recommended. In Josey's story, his early support led to friendship and that continues even though it has been several years since the critical incident. He is no longer providing peer support; he is sharing in friendship. Peers should always consult with their clinical director on their Critical Incident Stress Management team when unexpected circumstances arise. They should also recognize that crossing the line is an exception to the rule and not the rule itself.

The Roadmap

Whether the person you are trying to assist is cognitively oriented or affectively oriented (see comments section for chapter 8 of this book), sooner or later they will benefit from obtaining a roadmap about what is likely to happen to them and what emotions they may have to face. When Josey tells the Baker the story of the rabbit and gives him some insight into what it takes to survive and how things might go in the future, he has given the Baker a roadmap.

I have lost count of the number of times people have said to me something like, "If only I had known that, it would have made my trauma recovery so much easier." Or, "I wish someone had taken the time to explain that whole thing to me. I felt like I was driving a car while I was blind. It seemed like there were lots of curves and turns and I just wasn't prepared for them."

When you are giving people the psychological roadmap, you need to stick to generalities. You cannot make firm predictions about what someone might go through as they work their way through the recovery stages of the traumatic experience. Everyone is different. You can only tell them what commonly happens to trauma survivors. You should also pepper the road map with comments like, "You might be lucky and not have this or that happen to you, but if it does, then you will know that it is not unusual or crazy. It is a common way people try to cope with traumatic events."

Once people have the roadmap they feel more secure and they are not thrown totally off track when something unexpected arises.

If, for instance, the peer gives a traumatized person a "heads up" about some reaction that might happen and then it happens, the person will be able to recognize that he or she was forewarned. He or she will remember that the peer suggested that the reaction is common. The traumatized person will feel that he has control over it because the reaction was portrayed as a normal, although uncomfortable, reaction in other people. The peer support person can remind them that they had been warned about what might happen to them and that, although, unexpected, they are not far from what others experience after traumatic events. The roadmap helps them to see their ultimate goals and to look back to where they started so that they can see how much progress they have made.

Hamster Wheel vs. Persistent Replaying

Remember the hamster wheel concept was discussed in the comments section for Chapter 5? Everyone does "hamster wheeling." We keep rethinking an experience until we can categorize that experience. Categorizing is one of the primary executive functions of the brain. Hamster wheeling is considered a normal function when people have been exposed to a traumatic event. They need to find a category where the experience can be placed. It is uncomfortable not to have a category in which to store a traumatic experience, so our brains keep trying to find one. Hamster Wheeling helps us to create a new category, somewhat like a file in a file draw, in which we can store a new or an unusual traumatic memory. Ideally speaking, the new traumatic memory gets *associated* with other memories. It helps a person to psychologically accept what has happened and 'park' it in place in your brain where you know what it is and what will trigger the memories. It is important to know that a memory alone does not harm you.

Acceptance

The proof of healing is not an erasure or the elimination of the memory of a traumatic experience. Forgetting is not the object of healing. The essence of healing is being able to accept the tragedy and understand one' role in it. Acceptance does not mean we like what has happened. Acceptance and healing occurs if we can learn whatever we can from it even if the memories will always be unpleasant or painful.

In some cases, a person may have a difficult time accepting a tragedy if there is pending legal action or other punitive actions against him or her. The worry associated with potential legal, social, financial actions keeps the hamster wheeling going longer. Once the peripheral issues are resolved, acceptance is a bit easier to achieve. Healing can be completed even though we do not like the outcome of the event.

Acceptance of the tragedy and its effects is the healthier place to be if you compare it to people who get stuck replaying the event as described below.

Persistent Replaying

Persistent Replaying is not a normal function like hamster wheeling. Replaying, instead, is an attempt to deny or undo an event. If a family member was killed in an auto accident, another family member might try to undo that event in their imagination. He or she may try to imagine that the auto accident never occurred in the first place. They may explain the person's absence by claiming that the person is away on a training mission. Some people go so far as to actually destroy evidence of an event so that they can continue to deny the occurrence. They believe that erasing every aspect of an event means that it did not really happen. I met a woman once whose police officer husband was killed in action. She refused to sign a document confirming the receipt of a death benefit package. When questioned about this she told another officer that if she signed the document it would mean that he was really dead. She told the officer that she could not accept that. She kept stating repeatedly that he would be back in a few days. Her refusal to sign for long period of time was her way of trying to undo the situation.

Other people just keep rerunning the event through their imaginations. They rethink the event over and over like a mental

DVD player that can't be shut off. Persistent replaying occurs because the person cannot accept the outcome of a real event. It is driven by extended denial, guilt, and feelings of personal responsibility.

It has been my experience that persistent replaying is very much more common in people who have sustained physical injuries. When the Baker is sitting on the sofa due to the injury he is doing persistent replaying of what caused him to get there. It is hard not to replay the traumatic event if every time you move a part of your body it hurts and you get an instant reminder of what happened to cause this pain. If a friend died, but you survived the incident, and you are in physical pain, your brain will pick over the incident trying to find a different outcome.

When a person engages in the agonizing replaying of the event, he keeps running the event through his mind, not to categorize it, but in an unrealistic hope that it can be changed or undone. When those efforts fail, the end result is frustration, anger, depression and self-blame. The replaying the event, unfortunately, keeps a person from moving forward in his life.

Not So Fast, Partner

We have become an instant society. Just add water and stir! We have quick gadgets for everything. From next-day shipping to instant on-line services and from fast travel to fast answers on our phones and computers, our expectations are that everything can be done quickly. When it comes to processing awful events and a quick recovery from traumatic experiences, the brakes come on.

It takes time for our brains to process a traumatic event both cognitively and affectively. We, along with everyone else, expect that we can get past things quickly; that we will soon get over it. Emotional healing is a slow process and rushing it along before we are ready can set the stage for a monumental failure and plenty of future pain and distress. Take it easy when you are healing from trauma and loss. It can be a long process. Human beings are not designed for rapid processing of our emotions after terror and tragedy.

Some Things, You Never Get Over

People cannot get over or past some tragedies and traumas. Some terrible things are a life sentence and you carry them for the rest of your life. People can heal, but it doesn't mean they forget. Healing will mean different things to different people. It is not the same for everyone. There are gradations between what is healing for one and healing for another.

We talk in terms of "getting past" something or "moving beyond it" or "getting over it." Sometimes people use the word "closure" to indicate that they are over something. The death of one's child is an example of one of those horrible events that many people never get past or over. There is always a gapping hole where that living special and deeply loved person used to be.

People with the deepest and most profound losses have the most difficult tasks to accomplish. They struggle to intellectually and emotionally accept the finality of the loss. Events and losses cannot be undone. It is a harsh task to accept that reality. People experience emotions that rebel against the facts and peace continuously eludes them. Some facts can never be known and that clearly deepens the pain. That is a frequent occurrence in cases of suicide. Many people report that the quiet moments just before sleep or the moments just after waking up are the most difficult moments of each day because, at those times especially, they are flooded with the memories of person they cherished so much.

When people do heal, it is not really that they get over it or beyond it or used to it. They do not really find closure. At best, they absorb the loss and they pick it up and *go on with it.* They are never truly free of the burden. They carry it with them till death and there is nothing peers, or mental health professionals, or members of the clergy can do to make it not so. We are all limited in the face of profound, life-altering loss.

The Double Ds

Josey has frequently said to hurting people after a traumatic event, "You can let the event define you or destroy you, it's your choice." I say it in another way. "Life's tragedies and losses can make you bitter or better. The choice is yours." In some tragedies we choose to tap into certain strengths and powers that we did not event know we had. In the end the tragedies define us as a stronger and wiser person with more sensitivity, caring and love than we ever believed we were capable of mustering. In other circumstances we are crushed by the trauma. We choose to sink to our lowest. We get stuck. We choose not to reach deep within ourselves and find our inner strength. We change our lives, our work, and our relationships with others. We are effectively beaten and destroyed by the trauma we have endured.

NOTE: Copied below is a thank you note to Josey that arrived at his residence just before Christmas, 2016. A man killed two children in an automobile accident. Needless to say, the man had both short and long-term reactions to the tragedy. He was devastated and depressed. A friend of Josey' asked him to visit with the man and do what he could to help him. Toward the end of the conversation, Josey told the man that he could not explain why it happened and why the children died. No one could explain that tragedy. He used his Double D quote describe above. And by Christmas time, the man had learned to have the event define him instead of destroy him. The note was typed and inserted here. It is exactly as it was originally written. The name of the individual has been removed to protect the person's privacy.

As I sit to pen this New Years message, I decided instead of writing about life events in 2016 I would write about the things that I (we) have learned over the last year.
I have learned that whatever rug you are standing on can be pulled right out from under you with absolutely no warning.
I learned trauma upends everything we took for granted; including things we did not know we took for granted.

I have learned that when things fall apart, people fall together. I am thankful for the community we live in and friends near and far.

I have learned to stop asking why because God has the answer even when we do not.

I learned it is better to say... 'How are you today?' than 'How are you?'

Healing happens one day at a time.

I learned how to ask for help...and I have learned how much help I need.

I have learned that resilience can be learned.

I learned the ability to compartmentalize can be healthy. You cannot let a single event define your life.

I have learned gratitude. Real gratitude for the things I took for granted before....like life. I appreciate every smile, every hug. I no longer take each day for granted.

I learned we should all celebrate each birthday, you are lucky to have each one.

I learned that sometimes you have to listen...not talk. Some of you can appreciate how hard this lesson was for me.

I learned that babies are natural healers of the soul. Who does not love the smell of baby lotion, dimples with a smile and unending giggles for no reason.

I learned it is okay to feel overwhelmed and humbled at the same time.

I learned that good news always trumps bad. Focus on the good.

I have learned that with little knowledge or skill, perseverance can build a barn.

I have learned that there is nothing better than being a grandparent.

I really recommend it.

Thank you for being a part of our lives.

- JTM -

J. T .Mitchell / W. J. Visnovske

CHAPTER 8

Sister Mary

As though my father was taking us to the Promised Land, we rode down the gravel road listening to him talk about this place where he wanted to build our house. We already had a nice house that sat on a hill and my mother's father owned all the land around us. There were days, though, when my grandfather struggled with the demons inside him. Dad said that our new home site was on a hill and that our new home would be surrounded by tall pines and we would be away from grandpa.

Dad stopped our pickup truck and the dust poured into the cab. As the dust settled dad pointed to his left and said, "The land is up there." All I could see was trees but we all got out of the truck and followed dad down into the woods. We walked down a hill and crossed a creek and walked up another very steep hill. At the top of the hill were the tall pines my dad had spoken of and behind the pines was a field of uncut hay. It was a hot day and the smell of the pine tree sap was strong. My dad talked of the road we would build, the two-story log home we would build, and the pond we would have. It was hard for me to imagine that because I had never built a house or a road but my dad could see it all, but to me it was just a patch of woods.

I walked down the hill and up the hill and waited for the school bus. I could hear the bus coming before I could see it and the lights blinded me as it came around the curve. I stepped back and the driver stopped and the dust covered me. I was scared. No one likes the first day of school and especially when it's a new school. My old school was a larger public school but this one was a small catholic school. My teachers name was Sister Mary. She wore all black and her head was wrapped up with even more black with some white cloth.

Sister Mary was old and she had something wrong with her and her head shook a lot. I heard the kids in class call her Goose when she could not hear them. Sister Mary could see I was scared and felt all alone in this new place. She did her best to make me feel welcomed and I needed that. The kids in my class did not waste any time picking on me and my funny last name. As I rode home that day on the bus I cried inside. I wanted to go back to my old school and see my old friends. I walked the ¼ mile down our gravel road and never told my parents how bad I hated that school.

A few weeks after that, mom and dad surprised me with a puppy. She was a Blue Mountain Shepherd and they bought her from a man down the road. Since my mother was part Cherokee we named her Waya Gila, which meant "wolf dog" in the Cherokee language. My dad used some spare lumber from our house and built Waya a doghouse. The doghouse sat near the front of our house and like our home was surrounded by pines. The roof was slanted so Waya would lie on top of the roof sometimes like she was a mountain goat.

The days at school were long and soon the kids were not content with calling me names, so they decided to punch and kick me, but never where anyone could see the bruises. All I could think about was coming home and seeing Waya. I would get off the school bus and run the ¼ mile and meet Waya on her doghouse roof. I would sit on the roof with her and she would lick the tears from my face. Waya soon became my best friend and I confided in her about how bad I hated my new school. I used to run and hide in the wheat field behind the house and wait for Waya to find me. Waya would blast through the green tall wheat and when she would find me she would chew on my shoes. I never believed in magic but to me Waya was magic. No matter how bad it hurt from the name-calling, the bruises, or just trying to figure out where my place would be in this new place, one lick from Waya seemed to heal the deepest wounds.

Eventually the kids in my new school accepted me just like the chickens we raised. They were always hard on the new chickens we would add to the flock. I guess because I did not start with them in kindergarten and I had a funny last name it was just easier to pick on me than to accept me. I never blamed them or hated them but I did blame their parents for not teaching them better. At the end of that school year Sister Mary kept me after class. She handed me a wooden crucifix and said, "This belonged to my mother and she kissed it every night before she went to bed." She said, "I want you to have it and, remember, you will be fine." I was not sure why she gave me the crucifix because her wooden pointing stick found its way to my hands more than once and not in a good way. I took the crucifix and hung it on the wall in our home.

I loaded up the last of my belongings and said goodbye to mom and dad. I squatted down and petted Waya and got one last lick for the road. As I drove down the pine thicket she stood in the road and watched me leave. My new job was hard just like that first day of school but those mean kids taught me a lot about how strong I could be. It's not easy to pretend to be something you are not and that was my job 24/7. I pretended to be a bad guy in hopes of getting a bad guy to sell me illegal drugs. Problem was there wasn't a Waya here and no wheat fields to hide in. I spent many a day and night crying on the inside. I would make trips home and stop at Waya's doghouse and sit on her roof with her and get a lick or two.

Waya was getting old and starting having trouble getting on the roof so I would pick her up and put her on the roof. One Sunday I took Waya for a walk in the woods around our home. My long hair and beard did not bother Waya but it bothered me. The woods grounded me to the person I was, not the person I pretended to be. Waya took several breaks and she struggled to make the walk back home.

A few days later my dad sent me a coded message on my pager. As I pulled the pager from my belt I knew that message meant to call home. I called my dad and there was no need to tell me I already knew. Dad said, "She crawled in her dog house and died." Dad said, "I knew something was wrong because her butt was sticking out and not her head." I told my dad to leave her and I would drive home and bury her.

The drive was three hours and so far in my life I had never lost anything close to me. As I drove those three hours, the hair on my face consumed my tears. I took a shovel and dug a hole across from her doghouse and gently placed her in it. I took off her old worn leather collar. I smelled her one last time and rubbed the top of her nose. As I shoveled the dirt on top of her I wished this was a dream, I wished for magic but magic never came. I took an ax and went to a patch of cedars that grew behind our pond and cut down a nice straight cedar tree. As I swung the ax and cut into the cedar tree the smell of cedar filled my nose. I carried two cedar pieces to where I buried Waya and made a cross over her grave. I said goodbye to mom and dad and this time as I drove down the pine thicket all I saw was Waya's wooden cross.

My soon-to-be wife and I squatted down and puppies soon surrounded us. I loved the smell of them and even enjoyed their razor sharp claws. We picked one out. A friend of ours trained police dogs and he owned the father of the liter. A few weeks later we picked up our new German Shepherd puppy and we named her after an ancestor that was on her pedigree. Her name was Pascha.

I was still pretending to be something I was not and the days were no longer long, it was the years that were long. It had been a few years since Waya died but the pain was still there. My soon-to-be wife was trying to raise Pascha and when I could I would come and stay for a few days and once again I was getting those licks to comfort me.

I soon found my way to a barbershop and the long days and years became a memory. All those years of pretending to be something I was not changed me, not in a bad way but the love of a good woman and a dog was about all I needed to make me happy. We had to move several times and Pascha got to see the ocean and learned not to drink salt water. After many moves we finally bought a house and Pascha had a yard bigger than a football field. I took her deer hunting with me and she would wait patiently for me to return to the Jeep. I could hear her tail wagging against the crate before I said a word. I would open the crate door and the licks would come. I would sit with her on the ground and I was right back in my childhood pine thicket.

We came home from the hospital and several folks had warned us that Pascha wound not accept our new son. I squatted down and held our son in my arms and Pascha smelled him from head to toe and licked his new born face. We always had a crate in the house for Pascha to sleep in but left the door open. Most nights Pascha would sleep in her crate and sometimes next to my side of the bed but, on some nights, Pascha could be found lying on the floor next to our son's crib. One bright sunny day we placed a blanket in the back yard and put our son on it. As he played on the blanket Pascha lay down next to him and no matter what was going on she never moved.

I took Pascha out to relieve herself one more time and she struggled to get up the steps into the house. Pascha had aged and during the last few months she had several trips to the vet. I told my wife that I thought Pascha was dying and that I was going to pray she died in her sleep. I seldom pray to God and ask for anything. I figure God has a lot going on and why add to the pile. At 11 pm I crawled in bed and at 2 am I made the long walk down our hallway and I could see her butt sticking out of her crate. I dropped to my knees and cried. I crawled over to her and put my hands on her and she was dead. I guess my mind knew where to put the pain but it was too much like the last time. It was as though Waya's death was two days ago. I wrapped Pascha in a blanket and in the dark of night carried her to the corner of our yard. My wife held a flash light as I dug a hole for her. I removed her collar and placed her in the hole with the blanket. I placed her favorite bone next to her. I took the wind up clock that we used to calm her when she was a puppy and wound it up and placed it next to her. As I shoveled the dirt on her once again there was no magic just the faint disappearing sound of the clock ticking.

A few days later we placed a concrete statue of a German Shepherd over her gravesite. Our son was young enough that he asked where was Pascha. For him, she faded away, but for me, I longed for the licks from her. This time it was different. This time I had one life and not two.

When Waya died only my real life knew of her and when I returned to the world of pretending I could temporarily escape the pain. Now I only had one life and everyone around me knew of Pascha and even though I had been down this pine thicket road before it was as though this was a new road. I could not speak of her, but she was always on mind and when friends would speak of her I cried inside. The first time I walked up to the Jeep on the first deer hunt of the year there was no thumping of her tail in the crate. I sat on the ground in the dark and cried.

My wife, my two boys and I were surrounded by hyper German Shepherd puppies as we picked our new puppy from the litter. We did not have a name picked out but we decided to use his kennel name, it seemed to fit him well. If not raising two young boys was not enough I felt the need to add a puppy to the mix.

I sat at my computer and our new dog rested his head on my right foot. Our new dog is now seven years old. I received a text message from a friend that he had to put his dog to sleep, his name was "Max." A few days after Max died I received this email from my friend.

"It is a place where I wanted grass to grow. It is a place where I hope grass never grows again. It is a special place. A cool, resting place. It is dirt surrounded by lush green grass. It was also at one time itself lush and green. It is now a patch of dirt. As people pass by do they wonder how or why this place came to be? Do they know why grass won't grow there? I can see him killing the grass. He had no concern for my desire to have the grass grow there. He chose this place and killed the grass. Now it is a patch of dirt. He killed it. I hope grass never again grows in this place. He was majestic and strong. Brave and considerate. He was mischief and courage and loyalty. He killed my grass. He watched me water and fertilize. He killed my grass. That one spot he claimed for himself. He killed the grass and I never want it to grow again. If I stand there and see him there, in my mind's eye, my tears are so many that it will guarantee that grass will never grow there as they fade into that patch of dirt. That patch of dirt where grass won't grow is a precious place for me now. It has only been a few days and I caught a piece of grass trying to grow there. I killed it. I love that patch of dirt. Max killed the grass. He did it on purpose and he loved to lie there. On post. Waiting, watching, sleeping; just being a dog. He killed my grass but he grew my heart. That patch of dirt is now sacred to me. I knelt down and looked close and saw his fur in the dirt. He killed my grass and I miss him. I wouldn't trade one last run with him for the best lawn in the world. It was from this patch of dirt; where he killed my grass, where he would slowly get up and greet every passerby and walk a few steps with him or her and see them on their way. He listened to them all and kept their secrets. He protected them as they passed his patch of dirt where he killed the grass. He saw the kids off to school from that patch of dirt and saw them home. I miss him. There is a place in my heart that is now a patch of dirt—a place where grass won't grow. Every time I see it I am overwhelmed with the most beautiful memory filled sadness and joy and friendship that a patch of dirt could ever muster. I'm glad Max killed my grass. I loved him. I love him still. I cherish that patch of dirt. He killed my grass."

As I read the words from my friend I cried. I cried for his pain and my pain that seems to linger. The pine thicket and wooden cross are miles from here but I can still smell the cedar as I swung that ax into the tree. I can smell the fresh earth and see my wife holding the light as I dug the grave for Pascha. I can hear the crackle of the baby monitor as I dug the hole. My new dog looks up at me with and senses the pain. He gets up on his feet and licks the tears from my shaven face. As if he were Waya, or Pascha the pain seems to disappear with each lick. I run my fingers through his coat and the softness and his smell seem to calm and ground me.

A few folks have told me that if they had not met me they are not sure where they would be in life. I often wonder if I would not have had those moments on Waya's doghouse roof if I would have had the strength to survive the first year at my new school. I often wonder if that year at the new school is what gave the strength to endure the years of being someone other than me. I often wonder as I traveled the many roads from the pine thicket in search of my niche in the world if I could have left my wife and son behind without the comfort of knowing Pascha was their protector. I can't help but wonder as I have sat here with his head on my right foot typing this story to you will the pain be any less when it's his time? Will I be spared the long trip to the vet? Will he die in his sleep?

Sister Mary believed in me. Years later I returned to Sister Mary with my long hair and beard. I told her my story and about my job. I held her hand and thanked her. I told her that her mom's crucifix still hangs in my parent's home. I never saw Sister Mary again, but whenever I'm scared or down I think of her simple words, "You will be fine." I recall that when Pascha died a friend sent me a quote from an unknown author, "Until one has loved an animal, part of their soul remains unawaken." Our love of pets cannot be described in my words or anyone else's words. A pet accepts us for who we are. They love us when we fall short of what we think we can do. They are the first to greet us when the house is dark and everyone is asleep. The single strand of hair we curse that never seems to go away but comforts us when we are miles from home and it's stuck to our jacket. They guide those who can no longer see. They search for threats that can hurt us. Some are heroes and some are just a small patch of fur that makes a bed on our lap. No matter what their role is in our life they intertwine with us in their own special way.

As I type these words hanging on the wall next to me is Waya's collar and Pascha's collar. As he rests his head on my foot I feel selfish that with the love of a good woman and two fine young boys I need him in my life. I'm not sure if I need him or the memory that he brings me of those before him. I can still feel the pain from the loss of Waya and Pascha but with that pain are so many good memories and to be honest I'm willing to pay the price. As for magic, it does exist. Maybe not in the way we want it but in the way we need it. If you ask me, magic is the lick from someone who believes in you when sometimes you struggle to believe in yourself.

- WLV -

Comments Chapter 8

Shaking up the Memories

It is hard to read the Sister Mary story and not be touched by the love story it is. If you ever loved a pet of any kind, this story will shake some of those memories loose. With the memories may come some of the emotions that have long been buried. Emotions connected to people memories and pet memories tell us just how important those people and pets were in our lives. Sometimes old memories and emotions exhilarate us. Sometimes old memories and emotions can be distressful, sad, and painful. You may have some discomfort for a period of time, but don't worry, in the words of an old nun, "You will be fine."

Love: Get Some, Give Some

At birth, a human being is already a magnificent creation. He or she is a superb and awesome creature, but not perfect in every way. From birth until death, a human being is a work in progress. Each person requires precision fine-tuning, most especially in childhood. Like a blank slate, the human system awaits the writings of life. The body requires nourishment. Within a few short years after birth, the soul's moral compass must be set and calibrated. Then it is permanently set for better or worse. The heart constantly longs for love, understanding, and acceptance from parents, relatives, friends, teachers, and, very often, a pet. A person flourishes most, however, when he or she realizes that caring for or loving another, whether a human or a creature encountered along one's path, are the most significant contributions anyone can make to life. Everything else that is good flows out of love.

Other People Influence Us

The influence of other people on the life of a developing human being is extraordinary. Nurturing, caring, acceptance, trust, kindness, communication, encouragement and love can cause a developing person to soar to incredible heights and to achieve the unimaginable. The responsibility of caring for a child, therefore, is tremendous and it should never be taken lightly.

Just as the human spirit can be enhanced by the influence of others, it can be broken as well. The damage appears in emotions and thoughts and in mind and body. The destruction of a person's life is frequently caused by the harmful influences of certain people met along the way. Neglect, disregard, abuse, rejection, disrespect, lack of nurturing, and the absence of love, care, and kindness all can be highly destructive. Damage done early in life may reverberate throughout the entire life span. Without a properly set moral compass, a person can easily spiral out of control and crash emotionally, physically, morally, spiritually and behaviorally. Finding one's way back with a damaged moral compass is, without doubt, a very challenging task. In any case, there are absolutely no guarantees of coming to the end of one's life unscathed. Our paths, however, are certainly made considerably easier if we have been loved as children and adults and if we have learned to love and care in return.

In his childhood, other children bullied Josey. He learned tolerance and courage. He fought off the impulse to pay them back. He learned from his parents and from Sister Mary that not fighting was the more courageous and stronger position. Sister Mary told him over and over "You will be fine." His moral compass was set correctly. It was calibrated to do the right thing, not necessarily the easy thing.

As a young adult, Josey was in the very difficult position of living a double life. A great deal of his time was spent as an undercover law enforcement officer buying drugs from criminals who he eventually turned in for prosecution in a court of law.

If Josey had not had his moral compass properly set as a child, he would have had a very difficult time coming back from his life on the dark side, where he had to pretend that he was someone he really wasn't. Josey had several very positive things going for him. He loved his fiancé who he was soon to marry. He loved his parents, and Josey loved his dog, Waya. They all loved him. They cared and they were there for him. If you have someone or something to return to, it is easier to make the journey.

Cognitive or Affective Orientation

There are lefties and righties. People can use both hands, but they are dominant in one hand. Fine motor skills performed by the dominant hand are generally better than those performed by the non-dominant hand. Some people are ambidextrous. That is, they can, more or less, use both hands roughly equally well.

In a similar fashion, all people have affective and cognitive processes going on in their brains all the time. (*Translation: affective means emotional and cognitive means intellectual*). These psychological processes take on a dominant role in people as they process their life experiences. As there is dominance in the use of hands in right-handed and left-handed people, there is also a degree of dominance in mental processing. Although all people use both affective and cognitive processes constantly, some people are more likely to begin dealing with their experiences with a focus on emotions. They are *affectively oriented*. Others tend to begin their processing with a focus on cognition. They are *cognitively oriented*.

When Josey received the coded message from his Dad, his cognitive processing system kicked in. He says in the story, "A few days later my dad sent me a coded message on my pager. As I pulled the pager from my belt I knew that message meant to call home. I called my dad and there was no need to tell me, I already knew." His affective processing kicked in later when he was driving home to bury Waya.

Eventually, everyone will need to process both affective material and cognitive material to deal with the effects of traumatic events. Cognitive information can help to calm the overactive emotions. Cognitive processes remain cooler. Cognitive processes have to do with logic and reason. They analyze the problem and sort out solutions. Affective responses can warn us of dangers and generate effective defensive behaviors. They raise the alarm when threats are perceived. They can also stimulate our cognitive processes to work harder to sort out problems.

Affective Domain

People struggling through a crisis are hungry for something or somebody to reassure and encourage them. That is, after they do their best to manage a serious crisis event that continues on without being rectified, they may develop emotional exhaustion. That includes a feeling of emotional hunger or "effect starvation." Feeling emotionally starved is part of a wide range of disturbing reactions. They may experience, among other reactions, a sense of growing mental confusion, feelings of uncertainty and ambiguity, the loss of self-confidence and self-esteem, a loss of orientation, increasing feelings of anxiety, apprehension, fear, dread, guilt, and an overwhelming sense of distress (remember, the dirty dozen from the comments section on Chapter 6). They are alive and active in this story. Heightened emotions stimulate behaviors such as running away, hiding, withdrawing from others, and uncontrolled emotional outbursts.

You can reduce the effect of starvation by being present with the distressed person and by providing reassurance, encouragement, understanding, kindness, gentleness, and hope. You do not need to fix a person in a crisis. It is more important to listen carefully and do small tasks for the person, who may be having difficulty doing things for him or her self. The more they are functioning on their own, the less you should need to do for them.

Cognitive Domain

When people are cognitively oriented and in the middle of a crisis, they often become "information starved." They seek information from anyone who can provide it to them. The trick is making sure they get information from the right people.

Cognitively oriented people thrive on information. They can't seem to get enough of it. As long as the information is *accurate*, as *complete* as possible, and *timely*, people will appreciate it. Information, by itself, has a calming effect on people. When compared to a group of anti-anxiety drugs, information has a much greater positive impact on human beings than any of the drugs.

Cognitively oriented people are most helped when they hear complete and detailed information. Information, however, should never be "dumped" on them all at once. They need to absorb information in "bite-sized pieces." It is best to assist them by providing practical guidance, explanations of actions that are being taken by emergency personnel or others, and an understanding of what has happened and what is being done about it.

We do best to serve cognitively oriented people by helping them gather factual information. If we really want to help, however, we must surrender our need for control of the both the situation and their reactions to it. We simply don't have that degree of control over anything or anybody. The person in need of assistance has to be in control of the amount and speed of information coming to them.

Who Is Affective and Who Is Cognitive?

In most cases, you can't tell who is affectively or cognitively oriented when you first meet a person. A good rule of thumb is to introduce your self and monitor their reactions. Some will go emotional right away. They express worry and concern. A few may get teary eyed. Reassure the person that you understand their distress and that you are there to help. If the person is affectively oriented, he or she will tend to be upset if you start pushing information to them right away. Many times they "wear their emotions on their sleeves." That means, of course, that you can pick up on their upset, emotional state right away. What they hope for is that you will be reassuring and kind and acknowledge their distress. If the affective stage is prominent when you first meet up with them, start by acknowledging and validating the person's emotions.

If there is no evident emotional activity in the person and he appears "stone faced" introduce yourself. If he immediately starts asking questions like, "Is he alive? What happened? Who did this to him? How long ago did this happen? What are you doing about it?" then you can justifiably conclude that the person is cognitively oriented. Continue to give the person information in bits and pieces as you fill in the information.

The worse mistake you can make is to push information at an affectively oriented person. They will conclude that you do not care about them. The other side of that mistake is to be too solicitous about the person's emotional status if they happen to be cognitively oriented. They will become impatient with you if you try to dwell on how they are feeling or say too many emotionally supportive statements.

If in doubt as to whether you have a cognitively oriented person or an affectively oriented person, give them the first bite-sized piece of information and monitor their reaction. When they nod that they understand what you said, or say "okay," or ask a question, they are ready for the next piece of information. They are probably cognitively oriented. If the person appears to be uncomfortable with information, let them know that you are aware that they are undergoing a very stressful experience and you understand how difficult it must be for them. Show concern and sympathy and understanding.

Another thing that helps is to ask, "How can I help you the most right now?" right after you introduce yourself. If they say something like, "Please just tell me she will be okay." That indicates the person needs reassurance (affective orientation). If they say something like, "I need to know what happened," then the person needs information (cognitive orientation).

It Really Hurts to Lose Someone Special.

It does not matter if you are an emergency worker, a ranking officer, or an every day person not involved in emergency services. The loss of a person or a pet close to you can deliver a knock out punch that brings you down immediately. Among other issues, Sister Mary is a story about the loss of treasured pets. It is the story of a young boy, harassed by the other kids, who finds a warm friendship and comfort in the constant love of his dog. It is also a story of the loss of a cherished pet and the pain one endures when forced to move on in life without your childhood buddy.

The Loss of a Service Dog

The loss of a service dog such as a police dog, a seeing-eye dog, a search-and-rescue dog, a dog that assists the handicapped or a drug or bomb dog is devastating to the owner or handler. These dogs are not just family pets; they are partners. There are months to years of training and bonding between the handler and the dog. They spend hours together at home, at work, and in the car. In some cases, the handler owes his or her life to the dog. Some dogs tip their handler off to the presence of imminent threat. Other dogs take direct aggressive action against a perpetrator and subdue that person. In reality, a line-of-duty death involving a service dog equals a line-of-duty death to a military or emergency services person.

It Helps if Someone Lifts Your Spirit

Life can be awfully lonely at times. It can also be overwhelming and discouraging. All of us need someone to lift us up, steady us, and put us back on the right track. Finding someone who listens, who cares, and who encourages us is one of life's greatest gifts. Sister Mary was an old woman of few words who supported a lonely and frightened young boy. She encouraged him by telling him he would be fine. Sister Mary made a difference. She helped a child to shine in darkened world. She not only told him he would be fine, she helped to make it so. She also gave him a crucifix she cherished to remind him that he would be looked over during difficult times. He would be fine.

- JTM -

Chapter 9

The Circle of Life

My Dad grabbed my hand and walked me over to the hospital bed. He leaned over and said, "Uncle Leon is sick again and this might be the last time you will see him." "I thought he was better?" I asked. My Dad said, "The cancer came back." I asked, "What is cancer"? My Dad said, "It's something people get sometimes." I stepped up to the side of the bed, my face now even with Uncle Leon. Uncle Leon was my Dad's uncle but we called him Uncle Leon too. Uncle Leon opened his eyes and said, "I'm sorry I can't do anything for you." I never said a word, but just stood there, wondering what cancer was and why it made my Uncle Leon sick. A few weeks later, Dad handed me Uncle Leon's deer rifle and said, "Keep this in your room and when you get old enough you can kill your first deer with it." The rifle was as tall as me, but I kept it in my closet until that day came.

Before I could see the headlights of Dan's truck coming through the pine trees, that surrounded my parent's home, I could hear his old Chevy truck coming up the hill. I walked out the back door and was greeted by my dog. I kneeled down and told her I was hunting deer today and that she would have to stay behind. I climbed into Dan's truck and said, "Morning." Dan had been my best friend since I was ten and I had learned that he never had much to say in the mornings. As we rolled down the gravel road, the rusted out hole in the floorboard allowed for dust to boil in around me. Dan did not seem to mind the dust as I watched him shift his truck without ever spilling his glass of tea. We drove past his brother's farm and parked his truck back in a thicket of cedar trees. As the sun was starting to come up, we crossed several fences to get the place where we were hunting. Dan told me to wait on this one ridge top and he would walk out the

139

bottom and maybe run a deer to me. I sat on the ridge, held Uncle Leon's rifle and recalled that day in the hospital.

I killed my first deer with Uncle Leon's rifle. I was not sure why, on this day, that I grabbed his rifle and not one of my other ones. In the distance, I heard some noise, and looked up to see a big old doe standing on the ridge top. I raised Uncle Leon's rifle, aimed at her shoulder, squeezed the trigger, and got her. Dan heard the shot and yelled, "Did you get one?" and I said, "Yes." Dan and I had to drag the deer back to his truck because we did not have permission to drive back through the fields, only permission to hunt on this farm. It was a long drag, but meat somehow tastes better when you work for it.

At a later time in my life, I climbed into the bus and the Marine recruiter said, "It's going to be a light load today." I asked the Staff Sargent where all the other recruits were and he said, "Since there was that international incident, several of the recruits decided not to join up today. They are scared there will be a war." It was hard for me to understand why people would not take a stand for our country, especially if we might have a war. The bus ride to the Military Entrance Processing Station was long and the recruiter was right, it was a light load. After a full day of tests and questions it was time for me to raise my hand and promise to serve my country. Even with the cloud of possible war overhead, I raised my hand with honor and thought of my father and how he had served his country too. It's the right thing to do when your country needs you.

As my boys and I drove 13 hours to return to my home state, I told them that they would be hunting on the same farms that I had hunted on as a kid. My 7 and 9 year old listened to the stories of my younger years and the anticipation grew with every mile. I told them that we would be hunting with Uncle Danny and that he is not really their Uncle, but he is in our hearts. I drove though the pine tree thicket to my parents' home and the first thing I saw was a homemade wooden cedar cross and a concrete dog that marks the place where my childhood dog is buried. As I turned around in the field behind their house, I saw the monument where my father's ashes rest next to our barn, a sight that I never seem to get used to. My mother came out the back door and hugged her grand kids, a sight I do not see enough.

The next morning we drove five miles to Uncle Danny's farm and saw that Dan still does not have much to say in the morning. His 16-year old son looked me in the eyes and hugged me. My boys and I drove back into the field and passed the spot where I shot that big old doe some 30 years ago. Dan was able to buy this farm years ago and now we can drive back to hunt on it.

As my boys and I walked back into the field, I took a knee and told them that many years ago Uncle Danny had to work the opening morning of turkey season. Since he had to work, I drove 13 hours on my motorcycle so that I could take his son hunting and his son killed a big gobbler right here on this spot. I told my boys that it's important to help a friend and help a young boy make his dreams come true. My boys and I crawled into the hunting blind and spent the next 10 hours in there. We never saw a deer, but we had my mom's homemade soup and we made some memories.

The next day, Dan took my oldest son to another ridge to hunt and I took my youngest son to hunt on my mom and dad's farm. We parked in the pine tree thicket and I told my youngest son that we would be hunting in a spot where grandpa killed his last deer many years ago. I pulled out my father's deer rifle and asked my youngest, "Would you like to use Grandpa's rifle or yours?" He asked, "Can we take both?" and I said, "Sure." Then he asked if he could carry Grandpa's rifle so I handed it to him. We crawled into the hunting blind and then the snow started to come down. As we sat in the blind watching the snow, I rolled down memory highway. I wanted my youngest boy to follow in the footsteps of his grandpa, but we never saw a deer. However, what we did make were more memories that filled my Dad's shoes more than once.

That evening, my youngest son decided to stay home with Grandma and help her do things, but I think he was tired of being cold. I went to meet Dan and my oldest son at Dan's farm and then we headed out to the back part of the farm to hunt. Dan took my oldest to a ridge where they had seen some deer earlier, but could not get a shot at one. I walked down into a hollow but I had no stand or hunting blind to go to so I sat down next to a tree. The snow started to come down at a fast pace so I moved under a cedar tree to give me some shelter. The cold weather is not something I enjoy anymore having had frostbite on my fingers and toes when I was 16-years-old. However, as the snow covered my legs and rifle, it had a certain calming effect on me. For the first time, in a long time, I did not cuss the cold. It all felt good.

In the distance, I heard a shot, and then another shot. I pulled my phone out and waited for the text message to come in. To my surprise, my oldest not only texted me, but sent me a picture of the buck he just shot with his Uncle Danny. I guess the snow was melting on my face because water was running from my eyes. My oldest had now traveled down the road where his father grew up and had done it with a man I consider to be my brother.

Dan texted me and said, "Keep hunting, I will get the deer out." I sat there as the snow piled up on my legs. The flakes were as big as bottle caps. I looked up and down the hollow, but to be honest I could have cared less if a deer came by.

In the distance, I heard the sound of a truck running, but was not sure why. As the sun set, I looked down at the creek and saw a big old doe coming up the hollow. I raised my rifle and shot her. I walked down to her and looked up at the ridge where some 30 years ago I did the same thing, only now I'm a lot older and so much more blessed. Dan texted me and asked if I got one and I said, "Yes." He said that his truck got stuck getting the deer out so he had to go back home and get his tractor. I laughed and said, "Some things never change."

I stood at the top of the field and saw the headlights from Dan's John Deere tractor. He told me, "I will drive down the hollow and get your deer." When we met up, I said, "Back in the day we would drag it out." Dan said, "Back in the day we did not have a tractor." We loaded her onto the tractor bucket and Dan asked if I wanted a ride. I said. "No I think I will walk." The walk up the hill was a good one, but steep. I reflected on the days gone by and prayed for the days to come.

As I packed my bags my boys asked, "How long will you be gone this time Daddy?" I said, "Just a few days." They said, "Why do you have to go back to that place?" I said, "Friday will be two years since all the men died doing their job and Daddy wants their friends and co-workers to know we have not forgotten them."

As I drove to that little town, that used to not be known on most Internet searches, I thought of those who still suffer, and how I wish I had the answers to their questions. I walked into the station and found the Devil Dog sitting behind his desk. I wanted to hug him, but he stuck his hand out and I was happy with that. We talked about everything except tomorrow being the day that changed all their lives. The Devil Dog and I rode around town where he showed me how the town was rebuilding. We went to the place where it happened and, as always, he had very little to say about that day. I can respect that. We drove by where the apartments used to stand and now there is nothing; just a concrete slab with a homemade wooden cross that was stuck in a drainpipe to mark the spot where someone died.

In a tree, next to where the apartments used to be, there are several pieces of tin that have wrapped around a limb. It appears that the tree has accepted this visitor as one of its own. That evening, I ate supper with the Devil Dog and his family, who had learned to accept me as more than a piece of tin that blew in after tragedy had struck this small town.

The drive back to my hotel that night was lonely. You can't help, but still feel and see their pain. I saw the fear in the family's eyes that they had almost lost their loved ones, and the guilt for being so happy that their loved ones had survived while others died.

The next day, I walked into the station and was greeted by the Mother Hen, who was cooking lunch and tending to her flock as always. She asked me if I wanted to go the cemetery and visit the ones that they had lost and I said, "Sure." As the Mother Hen

143

and I drove out to the first cemetery, she talked more about that day. I recalled on the one year anniversary that she told me she was there the day it happened but, when I first met her two years ago, she never told me the details.

We walked over to where a friend of hers was buried and she told me about the conversation they had had the night before it happened, which still lingers in her mind. As she finished that story, with tears in her eyes, she told me what she saw when her co-workers and friends died. Those images haunt her at night. I stood there on that grassy hill overlooking nothing but farmland, and once again I had no answers for the questions that keep her awake at night. She said, "My therapist said that I need to get it out, but I can't." I said, "It will come out when it needs to, we all grieve and cope differently." In true Mother Hen fashion, she pulled weeds from around his gravesite and tucked those unanswered questions and images under her wings.

We drove to the next cemetery where she showed me where her two cousins were buried who had also died on that day. She walked me around the cemetery pointing out people she had known who had died in accidents or committed suicide. When she came to her parent's graves she simply said, "These are my parents and next to them are my cousin's parents." I followed her around the cemetery like a young chick and noted the ages of those buried there. I was never good at math, but it was clear to me that cemeteries are not for just the old. I think that for the first time in two years the Mother Hen looked tired to me. She asked me to drive her back to the station.

Back at the station, the Mother Hen introduced me to a new member of her flock. I asked the young man if he would talk to me in private and he said, "Sure." I asked him why he joined the flock knowing that many men had recently died here. He told me that he knew one of the men that had died and to wear the shirt, to wear the gear, and to answer the call was an honor. His sense of duty and honor in the face of potential danger reminded me of my own motivation to join the Marine Corps despite the threat of war. I said, "And for me, to hear their stories, of those they lost, was also an honor."

A few hours later, several of the flock said that they too would like to go to the cemetery and also back to that place where it happened. I was asked if I wanted to go and once again felt honored to be a part of this process.

We returned to the place where it happened, which is now nothing more than a vacant lot. They walked around that place like a bunch of young chicks looking for something to eat, but what they were really looking for was answers. I kept my distance and could hear them talking. The Devil Dog, and the Mother Hen were talking about who was where when it happened. It was then I realized that they had never returned to this spot as a group in two years.

During a traumatic event the mind does three things: it attempts to Complete, Simplify, and Categorize the trauma. By their own words, they were stuck in the 'complete' portion of the process. It was not complete for them. By the time we left that spot, most of us had tears in our eyes. For the emotionally wounded ones, those unanswered questions were still unanswered, but at least now they realize that they all feel the same way.

We made our way to the other cemeteries where the men took off their hats and lowered their heads in respect. As we loaded back up into the truck, without hesitation, the lights and sirens were turned on to show their brothers they are still thinking of them.

Back at the station, waiting on our arrival, was the man who called-in this event that killed his best friend and many others. I named him Lt. Dan in my head two years ago and over the last two years I've stayed in touch with him. He too survived the event and was emotionally scarred. I recall the second time I spoke to him and told him that his friend had died with you watching his back and that he was not alone. Many people die every day with no one watching their back and no one caring.

As the clock ticked on the station wall, it was time for us to attend the memorial service that was being held at the church. I asked the Devil Dog what he wanted me to do and he said, "Ride with me." As we pulled in front of the church, I realized that this was four times in two years that I had paid my respects to men I had never met, but I could relate to their sense of honor and dedication. The first time was the funeral, the second time was the one year anniversary, the third time was them being added to a national memorial, and the fourth time was tonight.

We sat at the front of the church in a reserved section; I sat with the Devil Dog and Mother Hen. I reached into my pocket and handed the Devil Dog the Catholic Medals and dog tags that had belonged to my father. I explained to him that since the last time he held them I had added another dog tag. A friend, who inspired me when I was a teenager, had died several months earlier. His son knew the love and honor I had for his dad so he gave me one of his dog tags after his death. As several folks spoke about those they lost that day, I sat there, statue like, trying to be strong. The lights were dimmed at the exact minute, two years ago, when this little town made history. Sitting to my right was the Devil Dog's four-year old granddaughter, whom I had named in my head, the Ram Rod Angel. She asked why the lights dimmed so I held her hand and explained, "we were remembering the men who died, that had worked with your grandpa." I don't think she understood, but she held my hand and supported me, as I tried to remain strong for those I had come to see.

When the memorial service was over the Ram Rod Angel said, "Get me out of this mess." I picked her up and carried her outside. We stood outside the church like we were a lost flock waiting for someone or something to guide us. The Devil Dog walked out and got into the truck, so I guess that was the guidance we needed. We returned to the station and the kids began playing, their young spirits easing what most of us were thinking and feeling.

The ride back to my hotel was lonely like normal. The day spun inside my head as I reflected on what I said and if I said the right things to this group of people who are still suffering.

146

The next day there was a dedication of a new playground because the other one was destroyed on that day two years ago. The playground was the idea of the son of a man who died on that day. The son told his Grandpa, let's sell hotdogs so we can raise money to build a new playground. They sold a bunch of hotdogs. We gathered around the dedication and listened to people talk about the dreams of a little boy whose dad had died.

We left the dedication and I went and had lunch with the Devil Dog and his family. During our meal, the Devil Dog's wife asked, "Why do you keep coming back?" I answered, "Because I care." In my heart, I should have also said, "Because there is still a need." I said my good byes on the sidewalk and even got a hug out of the Devil Dog. I crossed the street, that two years ago was covered with news reporters and people who had never heard of this town.

I drove by the Mother Hen's house where she was doing yard work. She thanked me for coming down and I said, "It was an honor." I asked, "What is the one thing that has helped you get through this?" She said, "Going to the station." I asked her, "If I could take some of the sting out of that day, would she want me to?" She said, "No." She smiled and said, "I know you are busy on new projects, have a family and a life to get back to, you don't have to call or email, but please keep the stories coming because I need them to keep me going." With tears in her eyes, and a heavy heart, we hugged and I drove off.

The drive to the airport was long and lonely. I had people I could have called, but I just wanted to process the last three days. It is crystal clear to me now, that if we think our job as peer responders is done after that first visit, we need to rethink that. We all process differently and as in the case of some of those in that little town, they are still working through it.

As I walked through the cemeteries, I noted that we honor those that died by placing markers there. But, what about those who survived? Their emotional wounds were almost fatal to their spirit? How do we honor them? How do we place a marker on them? By coming back; in hopes that they know that we, the

147

strangers, have not forgotten them on that day that they gave a piece of their spirit in order to serve our society. We should come back to honor the survivors as much as those who have died.

I told the Mother Hen at the cemetery that death is a part of life, but even when our loved ones are taken from us because their body starts to naturally break down, it leaves us in a daze. When people are taken from us by violent force or worse yet, while we are present when it occurs, we are left not only in a daze, but we are stuck with unanswered questions like, "Why did I survive?" I told the Mother Hen that technology has allowed us to keep people alive, but it has also trained us to become an *instant* society. I said, "The death of a loved one takes a long time to heal, but these sudden deaths in a violent way will take even longer." I told the Mother Hen that the answers you seek, you might never find, but in a letter you wrote to me a year ago you said, "Pick up the broken pieces and go forward again."

I'm back home now in the arms of my family, but that town will forever be a part of me. I lost no one there I knew, but I know many there who are lost in a different way. When my father handed me Uncle Leon's rifle, he was passing on a tradition of hunters. When I raised my hand to become a Marine, it was about honor to serve like my dad did. When I handed my youngest son his grandpa's deer rifle, I too was passing on the tradition of being a hunter. I've accepted the death of my first dog that still guards the home where I grew up. I've also accepted the death of my second dog that is buried in my back yard. This thing called cancer that I cannot see, has now taken more people than I can count on one hand. These people molded me and inspired me to become the man that I am today and I have learned that cancer is a part of life.

A friend of mine's grandmother just died at the age of 102. He told me that she died peacefully, which is something we all hope for. As we lace up our boots to serve our country, as we put on our duty belt, as we put on our firefighting gear, as we jump in the back of the ambulance, or hold the hand of a little girl, or hand a rifle down to the next generation of hunters, or lower our heads in respect to those that die naturally, we are doing nothing more than honoring those before us and completing the circle of life. It may not follow the pattern we had in mind, but it is a circle and when we stop picking up the pieces, no matter how sharp or dull they are, we stop honoring all those before us.

- WLV -

Comments on Chapter 9

Those Nagging, Unanswered Questions

One thing you can count on in trauma is that those who survive it always seem to have questions that cannot be adequately answered. Josey brings that up in the Circle of Life Story when he refers to the Mother Hen and her unanswered questions. She still has them two years after the tragic event that took so many of her friends' lives. Most of those questions she will have for life. Many traumatized people suffer from cognitive or emotional starvation. They need answers so desperately it can be psychologically and physically painful. "What happened?" Or "How did it happen?" are cognitive questions. People need some information and facts to help them with those. "Who would do this to us?" Or "Why did this have to happen?" are affective (emotional) questions. People need understanding and reassurance to deal with these. (The issues of cognitive and affective orientation as well as cognitive and affective 'starvation' are thoroughly covered in the comments section of Chapter 8. If you are not yet familiar with the cognitive and affective orientation in human beings, that detailed comments segment is worth a read.)

ACHTUNG MINEN!

I went to Kuwait shortly after the first Gulf war. I was there to help the Kuwaiti government establish a crisis intervention program for their crushed and wounded nation. I taught in the evenings and had the mornings free. One day, my hosts decided that I would want to see the damaged oil production facilities. It was, in fact, a very interesting trip and I was amazed to see the destruction wrought first by the Iraqis and then by Allied aircraft during battle operations to drive the Iraqis out. My Arabic speaking driver stopped the vehicle at one point and excitedly jumped out and motioned for me to follow him. I did. About a hundred and fifty feet up this sand dune we were climbing, I abruptly stopped when I saw the big red sign that said, "Achtung

Minen." I am not skilled in the German language, but I was thinking that "Achtung" meant pay attention, important, or caution. I had heard that word used in some war movie. "Minen" appeared awfully close to the English word, mine. The big English sign next to it with big black letters against an orange-yellow background confirmed my suspicions. It clearly said, "Caution Mines!" Just to be sure, I looked at the third big sign next to it. That sign had no lettering. It was a graphic that pretty much anyone could properly interpret. It was bright yellow background with a guy being blown up by an exploding round object partly buried in what was represented in the graphic to be the ground. My guide turned around and motioned for me to come up to where he was. I pointed at the three big signs that nobody could possibly miss, but he had. The look of astonishment on his face was remarkable. He spent the next twenty minutes walking backwards carefully placing his feet in the footsteps in the sand he had made when he climbed up the dune. I never found out what he had wanted to show me, but we both knew it wasn't worth the risk.

The greatest mistake for any of us in dealing with traumatized people is to think we have the right answers to their many and difficult questions. Those questions come from deep within the wounded soul. Interpreting the question is a complex process and the potential to be wrong in the interpretation is extreme. The surface question often masks much deeper and more complex questions. We don't do people any favors by trying to explain why someone had to die or who would do such a terrible thing to them. Worse yet, "Why did God allow this to happen?" Right, you really want to take that one on? Our answers run the risk of being frivolous, ridiculous, or, flat out, erroneous. No one is likely to be correct, never mind profound, in any of the answers they might come up with. We need to think of these very complex and painful questions like a minefield. Don't go there.

In Time, It Will Come Out

Josey read the signs of the 'questions minefield' and knew enough to stay out of there. He said to the questioning Mother Hen, who had a hard time getting her thoughts and feelings out in therapy, that in time it would come out. He did not try to explain the whys and wherefores of the questions that were hard enough to express, never mind answer. Our job, as people who support others, through times of trouble, is not to answer their deepest and darkest questions, but to be there and support them as they struggle to find their own answers to those painful questions.

We Are Not the Same

Every one of us experiences, responds to, and processes traumatic events in our own way and according to our own calendar. We all categorize trauma in our own way. If we cannot find a category, we try to find a way to pick it up and carry it and go on with our lives.

It is disturbing to hear people say to others something like this, "Well that was five years ago. You should be over it by now." It simply does not work that way. When a traumatic event occurs, people enter a period of crisis. One definition for crisis is: *a state of emotional turmoil.* Another way to look at crisis is: *that it is an acute psychological and physical reaction to a severe and overwhelming stimulus, circumstance, or an event.*

Finding Resolution

I always say to my students in my Emergency Response to Crisis Course at the University of Maryland Baltimore County, "A crisis remains a crisis until some resolution is found. It doesn't matter if it takes 5 minutes, five hours, five months, five years or maybe even fifty or more years. A crisis will always remain a crisis until some resolution is found."

Finding a resolution that allows us to park the traumatic experience in our brains where it causes us the least disturbance is not an easy task. The brain will do everything it can to complete, simplify and categorize the traumatic experience. If it can't do that, then the brain tries to find ways to accept the incident and the outcome no matter how terrible. The brain can't change what happened so it tries to help us pick up the pieces and move ahead. The brain is programmed from birth for survival even against horrible events with terrible outcomes. We are driven to survive even when we wish we had died.

- JTM -

Chapter 10

Boar

I lay there on the cold concrete and asked my son to hand me the socket wrench. He said, "Is this where Grandpa taught you all the things you know?" I hesitated and said, "Yes but grandpa was always trying to teach me things but I'm not sure I was always listening."

As I lay under the truck and tightened up the oil pan drain plug, I thought hard about dad. I was not sure if it was the cold garage floor or the fact he was gone, but I hurt. I crawled out from the truck and sat up and asked my son, "Do you remember Grandpa?' He said, "I remember he was in a wheel chair and I remember he was real sick." I sat up against the toolbox and said, "Would you like to know who your Grandpa was?" He said, "I would love to know my grandpa." I told my son to sit on a milk crate and said, "I will tell you the story of a man called Boar. It goes like this."

The small boy kneeled down in front of the window and waited for his mother to return. From the street the small boy could be seen, just about every night waiting for his mother to return from her nightly outings. The boy's father lived in the neighborhood, but spent most of his time lost in smoke filled places called taverns. The neighborhood was located on the other side of the railroad tracks. Back then if you lived on that side of the tracks it meant you were poor. No father and a mother who was gone all the time left the boy with few options but to get a job to help support his family.

At age 8, the small boy got his first job working at a bowling alley. His job was to set the bowling pins up after they were knocked down. From a crack in the scoreboard he would watch in envy as the families came to bowl. As the pins would fall you could see a little hand reach down and set the pins back up.

At that point in the story, my youngest son walked into the garage and said, "Grandma said supper will be ready soon. What are you guys talking about?" My oldest son said, "Daddy is telling me a story about Grandpa." My youngest son said, "Can I listen?" I said, "Sure sit on that block of wood because this floor is hard and cold."

I went on with the story. Soon the boy became well known in the neighborhood as a hard working young man. His name was William but everyone called him Billy. When Billy wasn't working he could be found down by the railroad tracks watching the trains go by. He would dream that one day he would get on a train and ride to a place that was better than where he lived. Billy went to school but as soon as school was over he would have to go to his job. He would run to work and watch the other kids run off to play sports. Billy never did play sports in grade school or high school. The money he earned from his jobs he would give to his mother. By the time Billy was ready to graduate from high school he had lived in 20 different apartments. All of those apartments were in the same neighborhood.

In high school, Billy met a girl who was raised on a farm and in his eyes she had the childhood he always dreamed of. My oldest son asked, "Was that farm girl Grandma?" I said, "Yes, that was Grandma." They dated for a while but Billy decided that he would join the Navy and see the world. While Billy was in the Navy he would send his paychecks home to his mother. She was supposed to put all the money into the bank for him, but she decided to spend it on other things.

After four years in the Navy, Billy went home. His mother had moved from the Midwest to the West Coast. Billy found out his mom had spent all his money, but she was generous enough to buy him a bus ticket back to the Midwest. Billy went back to his old neighborhood and got a job working at the local grocery store. Billy started dating the farm girl again and they soon married. Billy applied to a local cement plant and starting

156

working there. Billy and his wife soon had a daughter and after that most people started calling him Bill. When Bill wasn't working at the cement plant he was out at the farm helping his father-in-law. To Bill, this was what he always wanted. He finally felt like he had a family.

Bill's dream was soon destroyed as the real side of his father-in-law came out. His father-in-law was a man who struggled to be nice sometimes. My youngest son asked, "So that was your Grandpa?" I said, "Yes but we were never close."

Bill and the farm girl had a boy and, a few years later, they had a second boy. Bill worked a lot of hours so his wife could be a full time mother to their three children. Bill never wanted them to wonder where their mother was.

Bill decided it would be better if the family lived further away from his father-in-law. This would mean Bill would be driving an additional 50 miles each day, but he wanted to protect his family.

Bill bought a 40-acre farm back in the middle of a big pine tree grove and needed some help building his dream home. Bill and his two sons helped him build his home even though they were small. My oldest son asked, "How old were you then?" I said, "I was your age, I was 10."

Bill's dream home was a two-story log house and this house was on the right side of the railroad tracks. He would work an 8-hour shift at the cement plant, drive 25 miles and then work on his dream home. Bill clearly wanted his children to have the childhood he had always wanted. Bill had a special way with his children. If they acted like children then he was their father. But if his child acted like a responsible person, he became their good friend. Bill did not drink, smoke, cuss, or have any hobbies that took him away from home. He liked to fish but his true love was his garden. My oldest son asked, "Who taught you how to hunt?" I said, "I learned a little from Grandpa about hunting but most I learned on my own."

Bill loved his garden and grew tomato plants that were over 6 foot tall. Bill also planted around 300 trees each year on his farm.

Sister Mary, the Baker, the Barber, and the Bricklayer

Bill said the reason why he planted so many trees was because, "All I do at work is knock down trees, blow up the ground, and then haul the rock off to be made into cement." Bill said, "I want to leave the world better than the way I found it."

Bill was a carpenter, plumber, and electrician. Bill knew how to work on trucks and tractors. My youngest son then said, "Did anyone teach Grandpa how to do all that?" I said, "No he just learned from the mistakes he made." My youngest son said, "Like the first hunting blinds you built for me and my brother look a lot different than the one you built a few weeks ago." I smiled and said, "You want to hear the story or talk about how I'm becoming a better carpenter?" He said, "Tell me more about Grandpa."

Bill's children went to a Catholic school. The school was located 25 miles away from their house, but in his mind it was worth it to him. His children were also provided the opportunity to play in any sports that they wanted to. That meant a lot of driving until the children were of driving age but to Bill their childhood would be better than his.

Bill's life had finally seemed to be going right direction and then things took a turn for the worse. The month his youngest son was due to graduate from high school, Bill's work had a contract dispute and all the union employees at the cement plant were laid off. For the first time since Bill was 8 years old he did not have a full time job. Bill looked for work but no one wanted to hire a middle-aged heavy equipment operator. Bill's pride and self-esteem had reached an all-time low.

He found work with a free-lance archeologist and went out west. The job with the archeologist lasted for a while and then Bill called his youngest son and asked him to pick him up at the bus station. Bill had not been close to his youngest son since he had been laid off from the cement plant. Bill did not feel like a man because he could not provide for his family like he once had. Bill's youngest son walked across the large bus station but now Bill's face was covered with a beard and on his shoulder was one of those Army duffel bags. The smile on Bill's face told his youngest son that not only was his dad home but his old dad was also home. It was about 30 years earlier that Bill walked across this same bus station after returning home from the Navy.

A few weeks before Bill was called back to work a building behind his home caught fire and spread to his garage. Luckily, the volunteer fire department saved the house but the garage was severely damaged. I pointed to the ceiling in the garage and told my son, "That's why some of those boards are dark."

Shortly after the fire Bill walked out of the burnt garage and handed his youngest son a brand new camera. He never said a word but it was Bill's way of saying he was sorry for treating his youngest son differently for the last year.

That camera has broken twice and both times his youngest son had it fixed and he still has it today. My son said, "When we go back home can I see that camera?" I said, "Sure." Bill was called back to work after a year but for $5,000.00 less a year and he lost some vacation time. Bill's dedication to his work didn't change despite his feelings of betrayal by his employer. One thing Bill taught his children about working was to give 100% regardless if you like the job or not. Bill had become an expert on working at a job that he disliked very much.

It was about this time people started calling Bill, "The Old Boar." No one seems to recall why but the name stuck to him like super glue. For some reason, Bill liked the name so that is what everyone called him. My oldest son asked, "Is this why you like to give people nicknames because Grandpa liked nicknames?" I said, "You might be right but only the special ones get nicknames."

The Boar was trying to finish a project he was working on before a major storm set in. In a hurry, he cut his thumb off at the table saw. The Boar picked up his thumb and placed it in his hand. He wrapped a towel around the other part of his thumb and put all his tools away. He even took time out to close the windows, so the rain would not blow in. He walked into the kitchen and told your Grandma that he cut his thumb off and that they better go to the hospital. The doctors sewed his thumb back on and the Boar was unable to work for a while. I pointed to the back of the garage and told my sons, "Grandpa was working right out there when he cut his thumb off."

Because the Boar was unable to work, he was worried that he would gain weight. The Boar still wore the same pants waist size as he did when he was in high school. The Boar made a trail around their 40-acre property line and called it the "Fat Track." In the early morning hours the Boar would walk on the fat track. He would stop at their two-acre pond and feed his catfish. His favorite catfish was "Moby Dick", an albino catfish. The Boar would also enjoy the wildlife that he would see along his trail. Soon the Boar was able to return to work but he still enjoyed walking on his fat track.

My oldest son said, "Is that why you like to run in the woods now?" I said, "No, when I was younger than you, when we lived at our first house, I used to drive Grandma crazy because I had so much energy so she had me run around the property and I guess now I just like running."

Besides being a full time mother, Boar's wife also had some time for an occasional part time job. By now, all three kids were raised and Boar's wife took a job as a manger of a local health food store. The woman who owned the store wanted to sell it, so the Boar's family decided to buy it. The Boar never felt like much of a success, but his job made it possible to raise three kids and help buy a health food store. The Boar's knowledge of gardening and growing health food, and the personal touch given by his wife to the customers, made the store much better.

One night Boar's wife heard a pounding sound coming from the kitchen. Grandma rolled over in bed to awake the Boar but he was not there. She walked into the kitchen and the Boar was beating his head against one of the pine tree log walls of the house. She asked the Boar why he was doing that and he said his head would not stop hurting.

The Boar went to his family doctor and they started doing lots of tests on him. The Boar was soon admitted to the hospital and specialized doctors were called in. Weeks went by and the Boar's pain increased and it appeared his body was shutting down. The Boar's family doctor had a theory as to what the Boar had but the experts did not believe it. The family doctor believed that the Boar had Rocky Mountain Tick Fever. The expert doctors had never heard of a case of Rocky Mountain Tick Fever in this part of the country so they ruled it out. The Boar told the doctors that he recalled a tick bit him between his shoulder blades and he attempted to remove it himself but was not sure if he had. The Boar thought the tick bit him while he was walking on the fat track. After several tests, the Boar tested positive for Rocky Mountain Tick Fever.

The Boar was never the same after he contracted the fever. After the fever the Boar became more emotional. He would express himself more often and be more likely to tell you how he felt. The Boar recovered from the fever and soon he was back to work and walking on the fat track as usual. Moby Dick was very glad to see the Boar was back. My oldest son asked, "Is that why you always tell me and my brother to express our feelings because Grandpa was not real good at it?" I said, "Yes, grandpa held a lot in and I think it made his belly hurt."

About a year after the fever the Boar was working a midnight shift at the cement plant. The Boar was driving a dump truck about the size of a large house. As the Boar dumped the load of rock, he pulled the lever to return the bed to the body of the truck. When the bed is resting on the body of the truck, the bed also provides the cab with protection from any rock that might fall on the cab of the truck as the bed is being loaded.

The Boar assumed the bed had returned to the body and he started to drive away. As he drove away the bed was still up because the lever had malfunctioned. The bed hit a large conveyer belt and approximately 20 tons of steel came crashing down on top of the unprotected cab of the dump truck. As the dust settled the Boar's fellow workers came running to his aid. As they yelled his name there was no response to be heard. They yelled again and finally one of the workers had worked his way through the debris and looked in the smashed cab. The worker asked the Boar if he was all right. The Boar responded, "Yes."

The worker asked the Boar why he did not respond the first time. The Boar said, "I was trying to find my glasses before I crawled out."

The bosses at the cement plant told the Boar that he was going to be fired because he had done a half million dollars' worth of damage and he also completely shut the cement plant down. The union fought for the Boar and said that the equipment had malfunctioned and the equipment had been reported prior to the accident. The cement plant did not fire the Boar, but put him on probation for a year. Once again the Boar felt betrayed by a place to which he had dedicated his whole life. My youngest son said, "When that happened were you married to momma?" I said, "Not yet but we are getting there."

The health food store had become quite the success. Business was so good that they moved the store to a better location. The Boar's family thought that they might be able to support themselves on the health food store income and the Boar could be released from the job he hated. After 30 years and only asking for one day off, the Boar retired from the cement plant. The sad part was that he was so used to feeling bad about having to go to work that it took nearly a year for him to realize he was free.

The Boar worked at home and also helped out at the health food store. It finally appeared that the Boar was going to be able to enjoy his life. Then the Boar started to notice more than usual back pain. He had always had a bad back but this pain was more intense than ever. After several different doctors examined him, the Boar was told that he had a tumor in his lower back. The doctors did a biopsy and the tumor was malignant. The tumor had eaten into several bones in his lower back but they believed that with surgery, everything would be all right.

As the Boar was on his way to the hospital for the surgery he mailed his youngest son a letter. His youngest son read the letter in front of his wife and broke down into tears. The Boar told his youngest son, "If we never see each other again, promise me you'll find a job that you're happy in." The Boar knew his youngest son was miserable at his job just like he was at the cement plant. His youngest son went to work and told his boss he would be quitting in two weeks. His youngest son told his wife, "That if I have to put the Boar in the ground at least I will carry him to the grave and he will know I was unemployed but happy."

The tumor was removed and the Boar was told that as a precaution he should take radiation treatments. The cancer affected the Boar more mentally than anything. A lifetime of eating the right foods and exercising appeared to not pay off. His youngest son told the Boar that sometimes cancer does not care how you lived your life but his words did not help him heal. His recovery was very fast and the doctors said it was because he was in such good shape. The doctors told him to be careful because the tumor had eaten some of the bones in his lower back and a fall on that area could do some severe damage.

My oldest son asked, "So you got married to momma?" I said, "I first saw your momma when I was about your age and even though it took a bit for us to get married I loved her from the first time I saw her."

Over the next few months the Boar did a lot of soul searching. He was always a very religious man but it appeared he was asking God a lot of questions. Whatever the answers God gave the Boar they seemed to help. The doctors continued to test the Boar to make sure the cancer was not going to come back and it appeared that it was gone for now. His youngest son was still trying to get the perfect job but the process was very slow. His youngest son and his wife would come to visit the Boar and help him around the farm. It appeared the Boar was both mentally and physically recovered from the cancer.

A year passed and the Boar started to feel the same pain in his lower back. He went to the doctors and the tumor had grown back at an extremely rapid rate. This time it wrapped around four nerves and had eaten more bones in his lower back. The doctors said they would have to operate and there was a possibility that the Boar would be paralyzed from the waist down. The Boar told the doctors, "Do what you have to but don't tell me anymore."

The day the Boar was scheduled for surgery was the first day his youngest son was to report to the job he always wanted. The Boar told his youngest son, "Do not come to the surgery because there would be nothing you could do for me here." The Boar drove himself to the hospital with his wife right by his side. He walked himself into the hospital knowing he would not walk out. As the Boar removed his shoes before the surgery he said this to his wife, "Life as I have known it for over 60 years will never be the same after this day." The surgery lasted six hours and his body consumed 26 units of blood. Over the next 5 months there would be seven more surgeries.

My oldest son said, "Daddy are you crying?" I said, "No, I think a got a piece of dirt in my eye while under the truck." My oldest son said, "What do you feel?" I said, "I feel regret, I should have been there for grandpa and grandma."

The Boar never walked again and he made it back to the fat track but not on his own two feet. Over the years that followed the second cancer, the Boar had many different personalities as he struggled to live his life in physical pain. There were times between the pain and the medications it was hard to love the Boar. On one trip home the Boar's youngest son put a quarter on a fence post and shot a hole through it at 100 yards. The Boar made the quarter into a necklace and wore it every day. My youngest son said, "Daddy you crying now?" I told my sons, "Yes, because I know how this story ends." I asked my sons, "You want me to finish the story?' My sons said, "Please do."

The Boar's youngest son returned home with his wife and new baby boy. The Boar held his first grandson while sitting in his wheel chair. My oldest son said, "I remember riding on the back of grandpa's wheel chair and finally I'm in the story." The Boar struggled as a grandpa because he could not be the grandpa he wanted to be. The Boar refused to let his limited mobility stop him from being outside and doing things. The Boar's determination was frustrating at times but also it inspired others to never give up because he had not.

The Boar rolled out onto the pontoon boat in his pond. His oldest and youngest grandson followed him. As he baited their hooks his youngest son sat back and felt a sense of relief that his father was once again able to be a father to young boys. My youngest son said, "We have a picture of that day framed in our room." I said, "You are right and we caught our supper that night and grandma cooked them up."

The Boar's health declined and soon he found himself in the hospital more than he was at home. The years of poor blood circulation to his lower legs had caused them to rot. The Boar was sent home and told he would die in a few weeks. The Boar's youngest son would come home for a week and help his mother and then return back to his family some 700 miles away. After six months the Boar took his final fighting breath with his wife holding him. The Boar died in the house he built.

My sons looked at me as the toolbox held me up and I said, "Walk with me boys." We walked out of the garage and into the back field. I stood there where our homemade basketball goal used to be made from plywood and a semi straight cedar tree. I kneeled down to my sons and said, "Look around because none of this was here and Grandpa built it all. Grandpa made me and I made you boys. We are doing our best to make this world better. Grandpa said he wanted to leave this earth better than the way he found it and I think he did just that."

My youngest son said with tears in his eyes, "How do you just go on with life when you lose someone who means so much to you?" I said, "Grandpa did not teach me that one, but I think Grandma did, she just doesn't know it." I looked back at the house and through the kitchen window I could see her making supper.

I told my sons, "Look at her, she has to be the strongest person I know. Her life was not easy just like Grandpa's, but somehow she can see the beauty of the sun set even when it's a cloudy day. She took care of Grandpa for over 14 years and never complained. She is just as hard headed as Grandpa and at times it's frustrating but it's also inspirational. I kept that quarter I shot for Grandpa to inspire me, and others, to never give up. Grandpa came into this world with the odds against him but he never gave up even when he took his last breath. Boys, I know this story does not end the way you would like it to, but we are writing our own story now so we have to go on. We capture the memories of those before us and then we make our own memories for the next ones to follow. You always ask me what did grandpa teach me and I guess he taught me how to live life when it does not work out like you had planned, and grandma is now teaching me the same thing."

My mom walks into the back field and says, "I fried the fish we caught out of the pond, what are you all doing out here?" I say, "I was telling the boys about a man named Boar." Mom smiles and says, "Did you tell them he was hard headed?" I smile back and say, "Yes and I also told them about his hard headed wife." My oldest son says, "Daddy what happen to Moby Dick?" I answer, "Moby Dick is with grandpa and he feeds him every day."

The four of us walk towards the house and are greeted by my wife and she is still as beautiful as the first time I saw her. I turn around and look up towards the barn and see the monument in the field that holds my father's ashes. I'm not sure how we got here but we are here, just like I do not know how my father earned the name Boar, but we accept it. Though his death pains me, his not-so-perfect life inspires me.

Through the kitchen window I can see the table is set and they are waiting on me. My wife looks through the window and sees me standing there; she knows that I am lost. I look down at my feet and I have never felt so grounded to the earth, too grounded. I can hear the Boar's words, "Pay attention what I'm fixin' to show you because one day I will not be around." I say to myself, "What do I do now dad?" but he does not answer.

A breeze whispers through the pines that surround the house he built and I can feel him. I stand there lost in time and wait for him but he does not come. I look at my feet once again and my right foot takes one step forward. As I open the door that he put on this house I can now see the kitchen table. Where my father always sat remains empty but only in body not in spirit.

- WLV -

Comments on Chapter 10

Oral History

Like his Cherokee ancestors, who, for multiple millennia before him, told stories about their lives, accomplishments, struggles, and relationships, Josey engages in an oral history of his parents with his two boys in the story of Boar. And for us, we get to enjoy the written history version of his family's oral history.

The stories of our ancestors help us to understand who they were and what they contributed to the world and to us. In most cases our ancestors contribute so much more than some biological genes and DNA. Josey uses many aspects of the story of his father and his mother to drive home the main points for his boys. He links for them their grandfather and their grandmother. He tells his boys about the character of their grandparents and how they taught him to honor one's family and help each other in difficult times. He tells his boys that life was not always easy for their grandparents, but they never gave up no matter what happened. He focuses most particularly on the struggles of his father, the Boar. Through family conflict and work troubles and through injury and illness and the loss of his legs, he never gave up.

He then ties his boys to himself and his wife and discusses how their family is stitched together like an intricate quilt. The boys indicate that are excited by being in the story and knowing their history. The boys get to see how they are connected with the Boar and the other family members

Josey tells the boys how difficult it was for the Boar to express himself and that he stuffed many things way down inside himself. Boar had a hard time telling even his own children that he loved them and cared for them. That did not help him. It made him hurt more inside, mostly in his mind and his soul. That is what happens when most people try to stuff things inside themselves instead of expressing them to others. They bury it within the darkness in some inaccessible area of their minds and hearts.

Josey tells the story of bright spot in his relationship with his father. One day the Boar gave Josey a camera to say what he had a difficult time saying in words: I love you and I am sorry I have been so distant from you. Josey's boys get to see that family members can be hard headed and have difficulties in communication, but they can still love each other. No matter what, they do not give up.

The Pleasure and Pain of Family Memories

Family memories can bring us smiles and laughter and they can bring us heartache and tears. Our emotions can run the range from joy, pride, acceptance, and elation, to anger, rage, anguish, sadness, disappointment, rejection, and resentment. In general terms, happy memories bring about positive, upbeat emotions. Unhappy memories have the opposite effect on emotions. The memories and the accompanying emotions all depend on what experiences the memories of our families are built upon.

It is not all good for one family and all bad for another family. Every family has a mix of experiences – good and bad. The memories are also not equally split in families. Some families are more stable than others and some, unfortunately, are more dysfunctional. You will, therefore, meet people who have hard time bringing up any good memories of their family.

Many memories have a bittersweet nature to them. People can feel positive emotions when certain memories come up and simultaneously, the same memories can bring about negative feelings. It even happens that two people can look at the same experiences and have totally different memories and emotional reactions to them. We human beings are pretty complex!

Some family experiences were wonderful and individuals felt nurtured and cared about while going through them. Those memories, therefore, were positive and produced positive emotions when thought about later in life. Other experiences were emotionally painful. When people thought of those things, the emotions were more negative.

Getting to Know Your Own Family

I recently completed a history of my own family. It covered about a thousand years of recorded history. It was a huge undertaking with many ups and downs and it took many years to write. It was exhilarating in some ways and frustrating and sad in others. It was, however, very special to see the reactions of family members when they each received a personal copy at Christmas.

I am not necessarily recommending that you write a family history, but I am suggesting that you learn as much as you can about important members of your family. You can, in that way learn a great deal about your self.

When you are connecting with family members who are important to you, keep these lessons learned in your mind regarding your own family history.

- Family histories are never fully complete. They are difficult to research and write up even when exploring only a branch or two of the family tree. Attempting to do it all is a monumental and, typically, an impossible task. Focus, therefore, on the people in you family who mean the most to you and about whom you would like to know something.

- When you learn something significant about people in your family write up a summary after you finish talking to them. Write while it is fresh in your mind. You think you will remember it all, but details will surely get muddled and forgotten unless you have some notes to refer to later.

- Some elements of any family background are lost forever. There may be no records. They were either never recorded in written or photographic form or they were destroyed or lost through accident, war, moves, illness, catastrophe, or as a result of neglect. Records are often lost or destroyed or deliberately hidden by some members of the family for a wide range of reasons. Verbal and hard copy records are lost in death or if someone develops dementia.

- Some of your ancestors may be famous and can cause you to feel pride and honor. Some may make you feel embarrassed or ashamed.

- Be prepared, if you study a family. Some family members are not the best people in the world. Not all family members are heroes or people to revere. Some are mentally impaired. Others are alcoholics or drug abusers. Some may be criminals. Others may have been quite sick and still others died as a result of their own ignorance or carelessness. Some family members are abusive of others.

- Some members of a family view other family members harshly. The stories they tell about their family rivals may be filled with misinformation, exaggerations, and even lies.

- The memories of family members can be flawed and the stories they tell cannot be verified by either historical records or by other family members.

- Most families are not purebred. Intercultural and cross ethnic marriages have occurred for centuries. We are more like mutts than pedigrees.

- Writing a family history or just learning about family members is no easy task. It takes patience, persistence, time, and dedication. It also takes some courage because you may uncover uncomfortable elements of your family system. Only take the gathering of information as far as your interest carries you. Don't obsess about details.

- Finding evidence to connect the dots in our family systems can generate frustration when things do not go well. But, when we do find concrete evidence that leads us to an ancestor or clarifies something about certain family member, the thrill is incredible.

- You must always view your family history in the context of the history of the community or country that formed the environment for the particular branch of your family that you are following.

• Good hunting if you decide to explore your family further.

The Family Story

Stories need to be learned and then told to others. Each person and each family has its own stories. Each story can amuse, encourage, and teach. The stories of our lives and our loved ones present a guide for our children and grandchildren. We should make every effort to know our own stories so they can be passed to the next generation. Let's not miss these opportunities. Once missed, they may be lost for all time.

Zeb's Note:

Below is a note from Zeb Visnovske, Josey's oldest son. He felt bad for the parish priest whose father had just died. The priest broke down in tears twice during mass. Zeb, who is learning to care for others by the example of his father, felt that the priest needed some support. So he wrote this note to encourage the grieving priest. It is a clear example that children learn from the stories of their parents.

Dear Father Pete,

This was my idea to you to help you with your Dad. My Dad helps people with stuff like this. The book is by my Dad and Dr. Mitchell. It helps other people with these situations. The story "Boar" was my Grandpa. My Dad at that time was in that situation as you are in now, and the card is my Dads number if you ever want to talk to him about this. He helps a lot of people. I hope this will help you with your Dad.

from,
Zeb Visnovske

Chapter 11

The Option

I sat there with my youngest, age 9. We looked out the window of the hunting blind given to us by our friend Mike. The blind had seen better days but with some new plywood, new roof, and paint it made us a small home off the ground. My son's rifle was pointed out the window at the food plot below. A year ago the food plot was a patch of woods. With some hard work we turned it into a bright green patch of clover. Though our friend Mike has never hunted here we named the blind and food plot after him.

My son and I wait for the ever-so-graceful white tailed deer to bless us with their presence. My family lives from the meat from the white tailed deer and though I get frustrated when they do not bless us with their presence, there is not a creature of God I admire more than the white tailed deer. My son and I whispered. That moment, even without the sound of gunfire, will forever be etched in my memory.

I was soon brought back to the modern day as my pocket vibrates as if a bumblebee is in it. It's a text message from my oldest son who is some 800 yards away in another food plot we made and it too was once just a patch of woods. The text message reads, "Dad there is a deer in the food plot should I shoot it?" My response was, "Sure, if you have a good shot." A few minutes later the shot rang out and my phone vibrated, but this time he called and said, "I got her."

My youngest son and I packed up our gear and walked the road through the woods to get to my oldest son. The temperature had dropped, the humidity was high, and the sun had left us for the day. We walked the road that I remember, years ago, was not a road. My youngest had his hands in his pockets, his backpack on, and he did his best to keep up with me. I taught my boys a long time ago to only use a flashlight when it's really dark. Our walk was with the little bit of light the sun had left us. We approached the wet water creek and crossed it.

I reflect back to the evening a few years ago when I walked my mom and oldest son to a ladder stand nearby to hunt hogs. My aging mother climbed the 15-foot ladder stand and sat down. Her gray hair stuck out like an owl in the daytime but somehow they killed a hog that evening.

My youngest son and I continued our walk and I looked to my right and recalled the day I decided to sneak through the cattails with the wind in my face. The cattails danced and every sound from their leaves rubbing together echoed in my head. I looked just a few feet in front of me and it was as if the dirt was moving. As I took a second look the dirt stood up and the largest hog I had ever seen on the farm stood before me. His white tusk stuck out from his mouth and he ran. Before I could think about it I placed one rifle round in the back of his head. I stood there with my heart throbbing and my hands shaking. It was all I could do to hold my rifle. I pulled my phone from my pocket to call my dad and told him the story and as I held his rifle in my other hand, I realized dad was no longer here. I learned at that moment the mile markers of an adult life are the births of our children and the death of our loved ones.

My youngest son and I walked into the edge of the food plot; I could barely see the figure of my oldest son but I did see enough to wonder how these 11 years have gone by so fast. We walked over to the white belly of the deer. To hunters, this sight eases our minds that we did what we set out to do. We stand there in the dark and cold and admire what we have been blessed with. I told my boys this was a team effort. We cut down trees, we worked the earth, we planted the seed and we prayed for rain but it was the white tailed deer that blessed us with their presence.

The tall pines around us whisper a song I've heard before, but I never seem to understand the words. I feel them instead. They remind me of the pines that surround my child hood home. On those summer nights without air conditioning, I always felt blessed when the pines would whisper. I love this time of the evening. The world, or at least my world here, is in black and white. There is no color to distract what my brain is trying to make into a memory.

The pines all look the same and even though I love the green and brown pine needles, no one tree stands out more than another. I can identify my oldest son because he is taller and my youngest because he is smaller. The bright green clover under my feet and the broad green leaves from the magnolia to my left do not distract me. I can tell there is a breeze in the air because of the sound the magnolia leaves make when they rub up against each other.

My oldest told me the story of the how the doe stepped into the food plot and my brain locked on to every word. I could not see his face, but I could hear his words. My boys were cold, but I wanted that moment to last a while longer. Some moments go by too fast. As we walked out of the food plot my youngest son told my oldest son, "You are stepping all over my clover, walk on the edge of the food plot." I laughed out loud because this food plot is my youngest son's and yes it too has a name.

It's New Year's Day now and I reflect from this perch that comforts me more than any chair I have ever sat in. My seat is just big enough for my butt and my feet rest on a platform about the size of a truck floor mat. The ladder to my perch straps to the tree and twenty feet up is where my perch also straps to the tree. I have many nice five-foot by five-foot hunting blinds with walls and a roof, but even on cold and rainy days you will find me on my perch. By far, my favorite tree to strap to is the magnolia. I love how her broad leaves can block the sun, shelter me from rain, hide me from the deer, and she has a certain smell like no other tree. Today my perch is under a very big magnolia.

Most find comfort in the company of family and friends on the first day of the New Year, but for the last 14 years I have found comfort on my perch as I wait for the white tailed deer. I sit here and reflect on the last year and all the hunts that I can recall. I reflect on my life and my purpose for being here. The pines are alive today and not only are they whispering but the younger ones are dancing at the top of the sky. My magnolia stands firm but her leaves have a familiar song as they rub together.

I thought of my boys as I checked on them this morning before I left the house. As if they were still infants I covered them with their blankets and stood in amazement how they fill up their beds. My oldest sleeps in the bed my father made for me some 40 years ago. He removed the kitchen cabinets from someone's house and turned them into a bed. My father was not a carpenter by trade but he was good with this hands. My youngest sleeps in the same type of bed my father designed and made for me, but our friend, who is a carpenter, built his bed. I think the edges might be a bit smoother.

I thought of life before the boys and can't imagine what that would be like. My wife and I waited for years before we decided to have children. I became a man of God and Country early on and I suppose I thought I could change many things. Then, one day, ten years had passed. We discussed the pro and cons of having children and I remember her final words, "I want you around if we have kids." Now, as I sit here on my perch, it's hard for me to grasp how such an impactful decision can appear to be like buying a truck that comes in a two-wheel drive version or a four-wheel drive version. It's an option.

The sun is now overhead and I have not yet been blessed with the white tailed deer. I look to my left and see the old logging road that my wife and I walked as she carried our oldest son inside of her. I recall the names we picked out. When he was born the outcome was no longer a surprise, we had a son. I remember when it was my turn to carry our oldest son on my back. Once again, my wife carried our youngest son inside her. We again picked out names. I remember how the pines whispered their song and the fallen brown needles softened our walk as we carried our boys.

From my perch, I can see the pine tree that I leaned up against as I really cried for the first time exactly a month after my dad died.

I can still feel the rough bark against my face as I held the tree because I was too weak to stand.

From my perch I can see the top of the largest pine tree on the farm. I can show you the spot where I sat in the dark a few hours after I buried my best friend. As I leaned my back against the tall pine and was still mourning the death of my father, I asked the whispering pines how much more could I take. I look behind me for the white tailed deer. I see the edge of the swamp and I remember the day I accidently stepped in my beaver trap. As I struggled to use my special tool to remove the trap from my leg I cussed. I had quit cussing as a New Year's resolution because I did not want my boys to hear those words from my mouth. I'm confident only the beavers and God heard me that day.

I recall the day I was tracking a deer and the flooding creek got the best of me when I almost drown. I can see the edge of my oldest son's food plot and I recall the evening he shot his first deer and from that evening forward the food plot had a name. I can see the tree line where my youngest son shot his first hog and I can still see that smile.

I look at my watch and I've been in the tree eight hours now. In eight hours I covered 48 years of living and the last 11 years with my boys. Today from my perch my boys do not seem to fit into the category of an option but more a requirement for me to live a complete life with purpose and honor. As I look around in every direction I think I have felt, experienced, endured, and embraced, almost every emotion and feeling possible right here on this farm. From love, fear, sadness, happiness, anger, and loss but I have never felt complete. Even though my tiny seat hurts my butt and, like a prisoner, I feel confined to the small area I can stand on in these woods. The trees bring a sense of belonging to the most inner parts of my soul, but I never feel complete.

Most of my life has been about options, but today the pines whisper their song and for once, I think I know the words. It's clear today that without my boys, my life would not have a song to sing, the words would not matter and the pines would not whisper. It's clear today that I am a man of God and Country as I have always been. From my perch the white belly of today, the black and white of today, the song of today, and the memory of this New Year's day, is that in order for my life to be complete I need to raise my boys to be the next men of God and Country.

As I crawl down from my perch and touch the Magnolia I thanked her for allowing me to share this day with her. I look up at those bright green leaves and they dance in the breeze. I tell the white tailed deer that my boys, my wife, and I will be back in a few minutes for our normal New Year's Day evening hunt and maybe they will bless us with their presence. As I walk the familiar brown pine needled covered road back to my Jeep, I looked up at the pines as they are singing their song and I smile and say, "I guess I was not listening."

- WLV –

Comments on Chapter 11

Life's Options

Life is filled with options. Choose red or yellow or blue or green. Take this job instead of that one. Pick your favorite dress. Select a car. Some choices are minor and have little impact on our lives. "Do you want to eat Chinese, Mexican or Italian?" Some choices are major and life altering. Get married or not? Have children or not? Some choices are temporary and can be reversed when we change our minds, such as when we decide to move a chair to the other side of a room.

Most of the time we select options with a reason. Occasionally we are impulsive and even irrational. Occasionally we feel that we are forced into a decision. Some choices we make contain inherent dangers. That is often the case in choosing a career like becoming a soldier, a fire fighter, a police officer, a paramedic, a commercial fisherman or a logger (commercial fishing and logging are the most deadly jobs in the world).

One Choice Blends or Conflicts with Other Choices

The options we select do not exist in a vacuum. A choice here, and another option there, will eventually blend with and combine with other choices and options we have already made. Together our choices can form us and shape us and give us talents and strengths that would not exist without the blending of our options.

Some options we choose now conflict with, instead of combining with, other choices we have made. The end result can be damaging or destructive. When a married man chooses to get involved with another woman, the destruction of one relationship or another (or perhaps both) is assured. Some choices cause us regret and they cannot be undone. We can only learn life's lessons from them.

181

The Choices

Josey realizes that once he chooses the really important choices in life, like selecting a job, training in peer support, getting married, or having children, his choices begin to define his life. His personality and what he learned from his parents, friends and teachers along the way combine with the more recent choices and define the person he has become. This realization is depicted most in the story when he comes to understand the language of the whispering pines and concludes, "I guess I was not listening."

The Options We Select Make Us Important to Others

Josey focuses a great deal on the options he has encountered in life. He recalls the important people who have influenced him, especially his father. His 48 years of memories, like the whispering pines, speak to him quietly and reassuringly. He knows he is on the right path with his life and his work, and most especially with his wife and children. He finishes the musings of his 48 years and announces confidently that he will be back to hunt later.

The Whispers

At Option's end, Josey finally understood the whispers of the pines blowing in the wind. He knew his options were beyond simple choices. His life selections were critical to his life's fulfillment. The whispers told him that his wholeness as a person depended on his life with his wife and his children and on people whose lives he deeply touched.

We all have whispers in our lives. We may not hear them in the wind blown pines, but we sense them in the depths of our being. The whispers come from our souls. The soul is the principle element of our life. The soul is the spiritual core of human personality, intellect, faith, will, and emotion. The soul is the life breath of God as described in Genesis (2: 7) "And the LORD God formed man of the dust of the ground, and breathed into his nostrils the breath of life; and man became a living soul."

Our conscience whispers, "Do the right thing." Our minds say, "Think, seek, and resolve." Our hearts tell us, "Love with all you have. Give just a little more." If we listen hard enough, we may hear our souls whisper, "Courage, loyalty, truth, purpose, honor, and hope."

- JTM and WLV -

Sister Mary, the Baker, the Barber, and the Bricklayer

About the Authors
Jeffrey T. Mitchell, Ph.D.

Jeffrey T. Mitchell, PhD is Clinical Professor of Emergency Health Services at the University of Maryland in Baltimore County, Maryland. He is a co-founder and President Emeritus of the International Critical Incident Stress Foundation. He continues to serve as a senior faculty member for ICISF. He earned his Ph.D. in Human Development from the University of Maryland. After serving as a firefighter/paramedic for ten years, he developed a comprehensive, integrated, systematic, and multi-component crisis intervention program called "Critical Incident Stress Management."

Dr. Mitchell has authored over 275 articles and 19 books in the stress and crisis intervention fields. He serves as an adjunct faculty member of the Emergency Management Institute of the Federal Emergency Management Agency. In addition, he is a part time faculty member at Johns Hopkins University in Baltimore and he teaches the on-line Psychology of Disasters and the Crisis and Conflict resolution courses for the Florida Institute of Technology. He is a reviewer for the *Journal of the American Medical Association, Disaster, Medicine,* and *the International Journal of Emergency Mental Health*. He received the Austrian Red Cross Bronze Medal for his work in Crisis Intervention in the aftermath of the Kaprum Train tunnel fire. The Association of Traumatic Stress Specialists approved Dr. Mitchell as a Certified Trauma Specialist. The United Nations appointed him to the United Nations Department of Safety and Security Working Group on Stress.

Jeffrey T. Mitchell, Ph.D., CCISM
Clinical Professor of Emergency Health Services
University of Maryland Baltimore Baltimore County (UMBC)
Co-Founder, President Emeritus, and
Senior Faculty Member
International Critical Incident Stress Foundation

185

About the Authors
William, "Josey" L. Visnovske

William "Josey" Visnovske was born in the Midwest on a small farm to blue collar parents. At an early age he found the outdoors to be a place that he felt more connected to than the concrete and asphalt world that lies far away from his family's hillside farm.

Josey is a Certified Fire Investigator with the Bureau of Alcohol, Tobacco, and Firearms and Explosives. He is also a member of ATF"s National Response Team which responds to large scale fire and explosions. In his 27-year law enforcement career, he has served as a deputy sheriff, a city police officer, a state law enforcement officer, and a United States Marine.

He is an International Critical Incident Stress Foundation approved instructor in six categories. He also volunteers as a specialized peer support team member at the On-Site Academy in Westminster, Massachusetts. The On-Site Academy is a residential training and treatment facility for emergency and military personnel struggling with critical incident stress and Post Traumatic Stress Disorder. During the last seven years he has worked closely with Dr. Mitchell conducting research, teaching, and developing new concepts to the field of critical incidents.

At an early age, he was sent home from school for a three-day suspension. It was then he wrote his first story about the field behind his home. He soon realized writing simply made him feel better but it was not until he met Dr. Mitchell that he could fully comprehend that writing was a way of coping and processing. When Dr. Mitchell suggested they co-author a book (Crucial Moments), he was very reluctant to share his personal writing with strangers, but he eventually gave into to the suggestion. After the first book was published and he received feedback that the book actually helped people, he was glad that he did it.

Josey recently realized that he was ready to write another book that might help people understand and cope with critical incidents and traumatic stress. In this book he wanted to highlight and more clearly define issues that occur in most critical incidents. He dug deep inside himself and exposed his own struggles in order for the reader to learn from him and from Dr. Mitchell. The goal of this book is to form a solid platform from which people can help themselves when critical incidents find there way to their backfields.

Josey is a family man and his family is very involved with his work in critical incidents. He is a woodsman, an avid hunter, and the woods is where is writes his stories in his head. He has spent most of his life trying to fit in, but when he enters the woods, he feels he fits perfectly right there.

William "Josey" L. Visnovske
Husband, Father, Hunter

Made in the USA
Columbia, SC
26 November 2018